BAKED

EXPLORATIONS

BAKED EXPLORATIONS

Classic AMERICAN DESSERTS *Reinvented*

MATT LEWIS

RENATO POLIAFITO

PHOTOGRAPHS BY
TINA RUPP

STEWART, TABORI & CHANG   NEW YORK

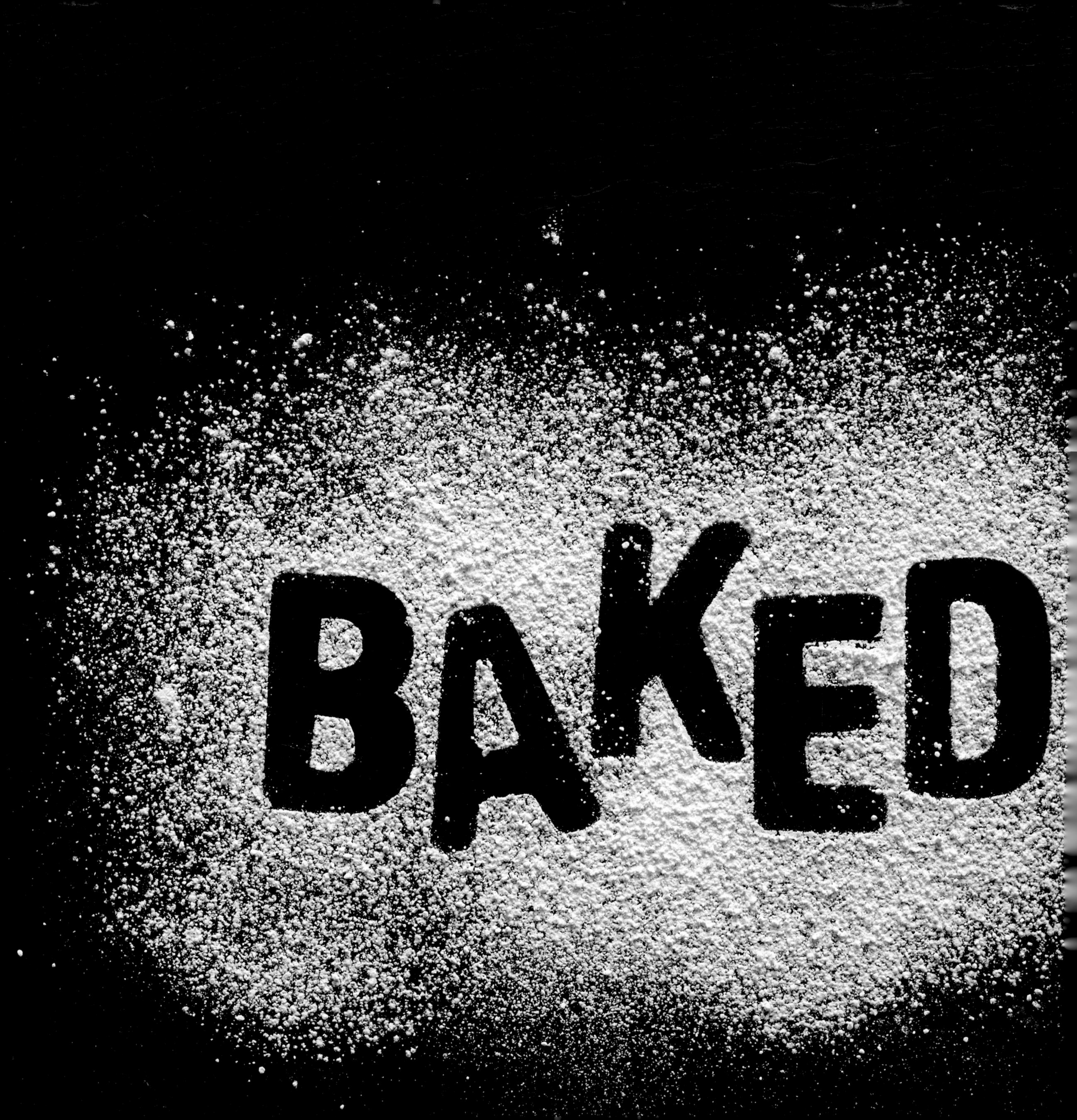
BAKED

Contents

Introduction
GETTING BAKED, AGAIN

OBSESSIVE-COMPULSIVE

I no longer vacation like a normal person. Or, rather, I no longer *plan* vacations like a normal person. Now, when cobbling together and researching the traditional parts of a holiday (destination, arrival time, hotel, and length of stay), I also include at least one dessert or pastry excursion of note. This complicates matters for both my traveling companions and myself. Whereas before, a simple ski vacation included the basic elements of planning, I now add a layer of complexity that most of my friends would rather skip. In addition to choosing the mountain, the condo, and the best month to ski, I might also insist that we spend a day off-slope in search of a much-written-up, much-blogged-about creamy bourbon milkshake. The kind made with homemade vanilla bean ice cream, homemade butterscotch sauce, and top-shelf bourbon and blended at the same location by the same family for many, many years.

Early on, I referred to my dessert jaunts as "research." I would tell myself (and my very tired and very full traveling companions) that I needed to "test" every chocolate chip cookie, every brownie, all manner of cakes and cupcakes, and every type of breakfast pastry to bring a deeper understanding to my development work at Baked or on the Baked books or for possible future concepts. Truth is, I would be eating my way through the United States and beyond, regardless of my occupation. It is my obsession and compulsion.

People often ask me if I ever tire of eating brownies (a signature Baked product). Absolutely not. What about chocolate chip cookies—don't I want to take a break from chocolate chip cookies? Never. I enjoy finding the subtle differences from bakery to bakery and state to state. I want to know why a certain bakery in North Carolina always makes a crunchy chocolate chip with classic, tiny chips, and another bakery in Oregon always makes chewy ones with large chunks of chocolate. Is the disparity regional? Did the cookie in North Carolina originate from a hand-me-down heirloom recipe? Is the Oregon cookie an amalgam, a collaboration by a series of pastry chefs who rotated in and out the bakery door?

My dessert "research" is neither conventional nor scientific. The format is loose, and the results are beside the point. I enjoy what I do, and I will always choose Pierre Hermé over Mona Lisa. My worldview is formed by desserts and the people who make them, and my true satisfaction is derived from finding pockets of regionalism in an increasingly homogenous America.

I'LL SHOW YOU MINE, IF YOU SHOW ME YOURS

There are obvious regional dessert specialties. The black and white cookie is nothing short of a phenomenon in and around New York City, while remaining distinctly off the radar in much of the rest of the country. Banana cream pie is a staple of the Los Angeles area restaurant and bakery circuit, yet it makes only brief and lackluster appearances elsewhere. Booze, especially the likes of Kentucky bourbon and Tennessee rye, is prominent in Southern desserts. Local fruits and produce are often directly tied to a regional specialty (i.e., blueberries in Maine, peaches in Atlanta). These observations are interesting, but it is the lesser-known regional subtleties that make my head explode. Dig a little deeper and unearth the treasures.

During Renato's and my travels for various food-related research (a great benefit to owning a bakery and writing a cookbook), we met people who introduced us to favorite desserts that had been passed down through generations and at church suppers and small town gatherings. These recipes, carefully archived, are perhaps hyper-regional. These are recipes that are typically neatly handwritten on brittle, yellowing paper and tucked away in Grandma's favorite cookbooks. An anomaly in a digital world.

We are always honored when people share these recipes with us (even, surprisingly, the Jell-O pretzel salad), and we are happy to share in return. It's an "I'll show you mine if you show me yours" scenario that has been deeply influential in our American baking repertoire, and we work daily to re-create or restore these truly great baking principles. Give us your vintage recipes, and we'll—ever so lovingly—turn them on their head.

ABANDONMENT ISSUES

Another subset of American desserts that Renato and I pursue with glee could be classified as Abandoned Desserts. Boston cream pie, Mississippi mud, all things grasshopper, and their equivalents are desserts that never

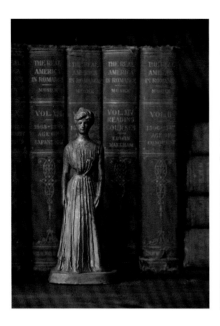

quite endured like the mainstays of American baking: chocolate chip cookies, apple pie, and brownies. The reasons for their gradual decline are varied, though still explainable.

Desserts, like fashion, are highly influenced by cycles and trends. If you were afloat in a sea of lava cake (aka molten chocolate cake) during the nineties, you were not alone. The dessert was on every restaurant menu (regardless of cuisine and price point) throughout the decade. As of this writing, spiking desserts with bacon is de rigueur. These fashions are part of a natural cycle. Lava cake will slowly fade into misty, dew-covered nostalgia, and bacon-flavored chocolate will become a fleeting trend, like parachute pants. When Renato and I dig through our pile of neglected desserts, we like to focus on investigating those beauties that lived through a few heady trend cycles and then were unjustly tossed to the gutter, like grasshopper pie.

We also look for baked goods that almost achieved classic status, like chiffon cake. For some reason, these desserts never quite reached their potential, and we place the blame squarely on the terrible versions people have encountered. After all, eating a substandard chiffon cake is like eating a kitchen sponge and sawdust sandwich.

Regardless, the Abandoned Desserts are something of a preoccupation of ours. We feel that it is our duty to provide some support to these old friends.

ABOUT THE BOOK

This book, *Baked Explorations*, is a tribute to beloved American desserts—treats and baked goods that are regional gems, fading beauties, or family secrets. It is a compilation of some of the more interesting items we found in our travels.

Renato and I set about looking for the roadways and history to all things sweet and realized that there is no direct route. Most recipes we found had been altered and tweaked by so many hands that one person's simple chocolate cake recipe was completely different from the next-door neighbor's, not to mention the recipe from the person two states over.

In some instances, we left recipes virtually unchanged from the version we were given. In other cases we performed a Baked makeover. This is not a compendium, nor a voluminous history of baked goods. Think of it as an easygoing road trip with stop-offs at the quirky and unusual monuments. Of course we included a few Baked customer favorites as well.

I hope you enjoy making and eating every recipe, and we encourage you to share a few with us.

EVERYTHING YOU NEED TO KNOW TO

Get Baked

KITCHEN TOOLS AND EQUIPMENT

MY KITCHEN OVERFLOWETH WITH USELESS, DISCARDED, AND UNNECESSARY, KITCHEN TOOLS AND UTENSILS. It is an archive of the superfluous, acquired many years ago during a brief, but painful, addiction to all forms of gadgetry. In an effort to help you avoid this brutal form of bread-machine and garlic press sadism, I have compiled a list of the most basic tools you will need for your baking kitchen. You can make anything in this book with just the tools and equipment listed below.

Baking sheets: I recommend buying heavy-duty, inexpensive, light-colored, rimmed, baking sheets. I almost always bake on basic aluminum half-sheet pans (18 by 13 inches) found at restaurant supply stores and various retailers (see Sources page 201). Generally speaking, the newfangled insulated and cookie-specific sheet pans are overpriced and not as effective.

Bench knife: A bench knife, or dough scraper, is an extraordinarily useful tool. Generally a 3 inch by 5 inch sheet of metal attached to a wooden or plastic handle, it is used to cut, portion, and turn dough. And it is extremely effective for scraping down and cleaning surfaces.

Brownie and bar pans: I always use a light metal or glass baking dish for bars and brownies. Dark metal pans produce unsavory, extra-crispy edges.

Bundt pan: Every home baker's equipment collection should include at least one Bundt pan. I use the basic 10- and 12-cup versions made by Nordic Ware. They are heavy, easy to use, and should last forever. There are also many decorative Bundt pans on the market (that turn out shapes like rosettes or castles), and you can absolutely use them for our recipes. Just make sure to grease all the nooks and crannies of the specialty pans to prevent unsightly surface breakage.

Cake pans: Keep it simple, straightforward, and economical. Use the professional aluminum cake pans available from almost any kitchen supply store (see Sources page 201). Stay away from dark pans to prevent crispy cake edges.

Cake turntable: It is much easier to decorate a cake (or sugar cookies, or brownies) on a rotating cake turntable. Heavy-duty turntables (which we recommend) are not inexpensive, but they are well worth the cost if you are an avid decorator. I would avoid the plastic versions altogether; they tend be flimsy and fall apart easily.

Candy and chocolate thermometers: Candy and chocolate thermometers come in many shapes, price points, and styles (including an incredibly cool laser version). For the beginning candy maker, I recommend the old-school inexpensive clip-on candy thermometer. Make sure it has gradations of 2 to 5 degrees and a range of 100 to 400 degrees F. Also, many basic candy thermometers mark all the stages of candy making (hard-ball, soft-ball, etc.)—this makes things all the easier for you. This type of thermometer should cost no more than fifteen dollars.

Cooling racks: I generally use two cooling racks when baking cookies and cakes so I have enough room for everything that comes out of the oven. I prefer the basic collapsible version (color and materials do not matter) that fits perfectly over a half-sheet pan.

Cupcake pans: The cupcakes in this book were tested in the familiar 12-cup cupcake/muffin pan made of light-colored metal. If you elect to use a different cup size, you will have to change the baking time accordingly. The basic rule of thumb: Mini muffins or cupcakes usually bake in half the suggested baking time or less, while the larger pans usually require time and half in the oven.

Food processor: If you bake and cook more than occasionally, I wholeheartedly recommend purchasing a large (9- to 12-cup) food processor. I know they are over-sized, heavy, not exactly beautiful, and often viewed as difficult to clean. However, once you own one, you will never give it up. It chops nuts and graham crackers with ease. It makes some batters, some icing, and pie dough with the flick of a switch. It's like an assistant, only better. Go get one. It has many uses in the savory kitchen as well.

Ice cream maker: Ice cream makers are fun to have around and experiment with. I own a fifty-dollar Cuisinart ice cream machine, and it works just fine (as long as you freeze the bowl ahead of time). For the more serious ice cream maker, there are more serious machines with larger capacities and built-in compressors (which eliminate the whole frozen-bowl business).

Ice cream scoop: The ice cream scoop with a release mechanism is a very important tool, if not a necessity. I use several different sizes of scoops to form perfect and uniform cookie dough balls and portion cake batters—not to mention scoop ice cream.

Loaf pans: As with all pans, simpler equals better. Loaf pans (9 by 5 by 3 inches or thereabouts) should be inexpensive and made of light-colored metal. I have three very old, very inexpensive, very effective, very battered Chicago Metallic versions, and I have a feeling they will outlast me.

Measuring cups and spoons: For liquid measurements, I recommend Pyrex (glass) 2-cup and 4-cup sizes. They're handy for melting butter in a microwave, too.

For dry measurements, I recommend a basic set of metal measuring cups from ¼- to 2-cup sizes.

All the recipes in the book were tested by scooping dry ingredients into the measuring cup, then leveling the top of the cup with a straight-edged knife (often referred to as the "spoon and sweep" method). All light and dark brown sugars should be packed tightly and leveled to the top of the cup.

For measuring spoons, use the most basic set of metal spoons you can find. They usually come locked together by a metal ring, starting with ¼ teaspoon and going up to 1 tablespoon. Measure all ingredients level with the rim of the spoon.

Microplane: Microplane actually refers to a brand. They make the long, thin graters most commonly found in commercial and home kitchens. At home, I use one grater strictly for spices and another strictly for zesting fruit and, if need be, grating cheese. Do not be tempted to purchase a specialized "zesting" tool; the Microplane is more practical and has many more uses.

Microwave oven: I know the microwave oven is frowned upon in many foodie kitchens; however, I am not ashamed to say that I use mine constantly. It melts chocolate, reheats coffee, and makes boiling water for tea a cinch. To melt chocolate (or butter) in the microwave, use short bursts of low power, regularly removing the ingredient to stir it, then repeating the process until it is fully melted. If you don't have a microwave, no worries; you can melt butter and chocolate in a double boiler.

Mixing bowls: You should own a three-to-five-bowl set of spouted nesting mixing bowls, preferably made of melamine. Melamine bowls are lightweight, super cheap, and easy to clean (I hardly use my old ceramic bowls, but I just can't stand to part with them).

Parchment paper: Parchment paper is essential to the home baker. I use it to line cookie sheets, cake pans, and loaf pans. It keeps things from sticking, and it is a much less messy option than cooking sprays and other grease-containing items (in particular that horrible flour spray). If you are baking cookies, you can reuse the parchment paper at least once. I find that silicone baking sheet liners don't produce the same kind of browning as parchment does.

Pie plates or tins: You can bake a pie in almost any pie plate or tin, but I am partial to metal and Pyrex glass. Disposable tins generally produce a soggier crust, and ceramic pie plates, while by far the most attractive, tend to conduct heat unevenly (often due to the make and age of the pan).

Pie weights: Pie weights help the dough hold its shape and prevent it from shrinking while baking. You can buy specially made pie weights from most kitchen stores or save a few dollars and use dried beans.

Skillets: I highly recommend getting a set (about three sizes) of cast-iron skillets. I found mine at a garage sale. They were inexpensive and already seasoned (a huge plus to purchasing used cast-iron ware), and I swear they are easier to clean than many more expensive pans. Additionally, I like the chewy edges they produce on both the cheese grits (page 35) and the chocolate skillet cake (page 147) in this book.

Spatulas: You should own several high-heat spatulas in a variety of shapes and sizes. They are essential for scraping down bowls, mixing light batters, and folding egg whites.

I also have offset spatulas—several small metal ones—for detail-oriented jobs like smoothing batters into baking pans, loosening cakes from the sides of pans, removing the first brownie, and swirling or marbling batters.

Standing mixer: Even though a standing electric mixer is big and a bit expensive, every home baker or baking enthusiast should have one with at least the three basic attachments: whisk, paddle, and dough hook. I have had my KitchenAid mixer for thirteen years, and it has never given me one problem.

Tart pans: I use several sizes of tart pans in the book for variety; however, you do not have to own this many to use the recipes (all the tart recipes herein offer pan substitutions where applicable). Tart pans have a removable bottom that makes it easier to remove the tart from its pan. When storing mini tart pans, we suggest layering them between sheets of paper towels or parchment paper to make sure they do not stick together while nesting.

Whisk: Home chefs should not worry themselves about owning the many varied types of whisks on the market. I used a basic wire whisk with a wooden handle (medium to large size will do) for every recipe that calls for whisking. These are great tools for combining dry ingredients (mixing flour, baking soda, and salt together, for instance), but do not use your whisk as an all-purpose stirring device (a silicone spatula works better); you can accidentally whisk too much air into your batters.

TERMS AND BRAND RECOMMENDATIONS

CHOCOLATE

It is imperative when making a chocolate-based dessert to use the best possible chocolate. If you plan on doing a lot of baking, it may be more cost-effective to purchase larger blocks of chocolate online or at local specialty stores. Luckily, in recent years, it has gotten easier to find good-quality chocolate at even the supermarket. The recipes in this book were tested using Callebaut Divine and Scharffen Berger chocolate, and I highly recommend both.

Of course, there are many other wonderful brands of chocolate to choose from, and as you get more familiar with them, you will start to align yourself with a few favorites. See Sources section (page 201) for a complete list of where to buy them.

Chocolate percentages: The percentage label on a bar of chocolate is confusing. One brand's 64 percent chocolate bar is often completely different from another brand's 64 percent bar. The percentage is really referring to the cocoa mass in the bar itself, but the proportions of sugar, milk solids, and any other ingredients can be wildly different. While I could write an entire chapter on this subject, it is perhaps easier to recommend the following bars for this book's recipes (see chart at right).

Cocoa powder: Every recipe in this book is made with Valrhona cocoa powder. It is deep, dark, and delicious. Don't get too caught up in the Dutched (cocoa powder treated with alkali) versus natural debate. Instead, pay more attention to the color and smell of the cocoa powder. Some mass-produced cocoas are almost gray—avoid them. If you can't find Valrhona, look for a dark-colored cocoa. I never use sweetened cocoa in this book (or for that matter, any other time).

IF A RECIPE CALLS FOR A DARK CHOCOLATE OF 60 TO 72 PERCENT, USE ANY OF THE FOLLOWING:

Scharffen Berger's Home Baking Bar 62% (found in most supermarkets)

✳

Scharffen Berger's Home Baking Bar 70% (found in most supermarkets)

✳

Callebaut Chocolate Block 60% (found in specialty markets—often chopped and repackaged by the market)

✳

Callebaut Chocolate Block 70% (found in specialty markets—often chopped and repackaged by the market)

✳

Divine 70% Dark Chocolate (Fair Trade)

IF A RECIPE CALLS FOR A MILK CHOCOLATE, USE ANY OF THE FOLLOWING:

Jacques Torres Milk Chocolate Bar (found in specialty markets and online)

✳

Scharffen Berger Milk Chocolate Bar 41% (found in most supermarkets)

Melting chocolate in a double boiler: A double boiler is a great way to melt chocolate or chocolate and butter together. To create one, you need a medium-sized pan or saucepan filled with water, and a (preferably metal) bowl that will sit partway inside the pan without touching the water. The chocolate (or delicate sauce) goes in the top pan, and the idea is that you are less apt to burn chocolate in this manner. Most double-boilers are warmed over low to low-medium heat.

Coffee Extract: Pure coffee extract is essentially coffee in concentrated form, and it is usually found in the baking section of most supermarkets. Nielsen Massey makes a wonderful version that imparts a smooth, never bitter, coffee taste. I use it in both the Chocolate Coffee Cake (page 155) and the Coffee Ice Cream (page 181), though you will find many other uses for it, too (like whipped cream, marshmallows, or hot fudge, for example).

Vanilla Paste: I am a big fan of Neilsen Massey's Madagascar Bourbon Pure Vanilla Bean Paste. The paste is thick and fragrant and contains real vanilla bean seeds that give light-colored frostings, fillings, and icings a wonderful speckled appearance. Generally speaking, vanilla bean paste is slightly more concentrated than extract but it can be substituted evenly with pure vanilla extract. You could also use slightly less paste.

Salt: In recent years there has been an explosion in salt sophistication. Salt now comes in many forms, sizes, and colors. In order to streamline the recipes in this book, I broke down salt into two categories.

✻ Salt: When I refer to salt in the book's recipes, I mean kosher salt. However, you can easily substitute table or iodized salt without a fear of ruining any recipe.

✻ Sea Salt/Fleur de Sel: In the instances when I refer to fleur de sel or sea salt, I suggest using a fine-grained (or if it is your want, slightly chunky) fleur de sel. Lately, I have been partial to Le Saunier de Camargue brand (easily found on the Internet or at gourmet markets).

TWO POWDERED FLAVORINGS

Though I have been playing with various flavored powders of late (I was given a few jars of flavored powders that look much better than they taste), I am still uniquely partial to my tried-and-true standbys: instant espresso powder and malted milk powder.

Instant espresso powder: This is not interchangeable with ground espresso beans. Instant espresso powder is intended to dissolve easily and is great for most baking applications. It can be is used to cut sweetness, accentuate chocolate flavor, and heighten the coffee-like taste of your pastries. Ground espresso beans will not dissolve and can give your baked goods a grainy texture. I used Medaglia d'Oro brand espresso powder in testing all these recipes.

Malted milk powder: Primarily still used to make soda-fountain drinks, this is one of our favorite ingredients. We think its tangy, nutty flavor enhances both vanilla- and chocolate-based desserts. My favorite brand is Carnation malt, which is carried in most grocery stores, but if you can't find that, Ovaltine chocolate malt drink mix can be used as well.

TWO IMPORTANT TECHNIQUES

The world of pastry relies heavily on a vast array of proper "techniques." My pastry world, and this book, are dominated by these two: folding and sifting.

Folding: When a recipe calls for folding, this means the act of gently mixing two parts of a batter together—no fast stirring, no whisking. The best way to do it is to use a rubber or silicone spatula and concentrate on turning the bottom part of the batter (often the heavier part) into the top part of the batter (often the lighter part) by scraping the sides of the bowl, then sweeping and twisting inward.

Sifting: Only a few recipes in this book require dry ingredients to be sifted. Sifting is the act of adding air to the dry ingredients to produce lighter cakes and baked goods. To do it, I recommend shaking the ingredients through a large sieve. Sieves are less expensive and easier to clean than the special sifting knickknacks on the market today. Besides, they have many other uses, while a sifter has only one.

BREAKFAST

Breakfast, or the concept of a "proper breakfast," can be unpredictable. I like it that way. When I feel inspired, I like rummaging around the pantry and refrigerator for unexpected muffin, scone, or pancake ingredients. I might use up some fresh fruit, chop some chocolate, stir in a bit of brandy, or break apart a stale baguette. When I am feeling less ambitious, I might just reheat leftover macaroni and cheese, or grab a bagel from the local deli, or both. I leave myself open to either option—I consider myself a breakfast optimist, and I never plan in advance.

It's not that I am blasé about breakfast. Actually, I am quite a breakfast advocate; I just never structure the meal like I might a lunch for friends or a large dinner party. I have never "dressed" for breakfast (a frightening idea!), and I don't enjoy the idea of sitting formally at a table in the morning. I prefer to fly solo for my first meal of the day, and most likely I am hunched over the morning news, be it on my laptop or the daily paper.

My carefree roll-out-of-bed-and-grab-your-own-breakfast attitude is largely a part of my upbringing. Mom encouraged the scour-and-devour breakfast scenario that still is part my daily routine. On occasion we were treated to last-minute innovations like a spruced-up muffin mix (usually loaded with butterscotch or chocolate chips) or a pancake burdened with more toppings than a tricked-out ice cream sundae. Other times, it was a simple store-bought, and probably not very good, coffee cake. My breakfast never looked like the hearty abundance of a tweaked-and-Photoshopped Denny's picture menu.

While digging for this book, I unearthed more recipes for breakfast than any other section. People are passionate about their first meal of the day, and the nostalgia runs deep—deeper than with most recipes. I whittled the written and oral submissions down, keeping to the sweeter side of things, and edited them down again by preserving the items that felt the most homey without being too kitsch. I can honestly say that I had the hardest time regulating myself with breakfast during the book's testing phase. One time I lost self-control, nearly consuming half a loaf of Monkey Bubble Bread all by my lonesome. The other recipes in this chapter are equally delicious. I still daydream about the Double-Chocolate Loaf with Peanut Butter Cream Cheese Spread. It is a rewarding and handsome breakfast loaf with a sinful flair. Mom's Olive Oil Orange Bundt is coffee-klatch heaven, and the Malted Waffles are a great excuse to use your waffle iron. If you are one of those rare anti-sweet breakfast people, I recommend the Baked Cheese Grits. Actually, I recommend the cheese grits no matter what. Have a great breakfast.

MONKEY BUBBLE BREAD

I SUGGEST ONLY MAKING THIS FROM-SCRATCH BREAD IF YOU ARE HAVING A LARGE GATHERING. Otherwise, you could end up (like me) eating more than you should. Simply put, this is addictive stuff. I liken these warm, gooey bread balls to the most amazing glazed doughnut hole you have ever had. There are several recipes floating about for monkey bread that use canned biscuit dough, but I ask you to kindly refrain from this expedient fix because the result won't be as tasty, and it is more expensive. The origin of the name monkey bread or bubble bread is quite hard to pinpoint, and while many dubious answers exist (the bread resembles a monkey puzzle tree or monkeys love to pull things apart), none of them are definitive, and some are cloyingly cute. I hate cloyingly cute. Suffice it to say that the source of the name is just one of life's great mysteries, and we should leave it at that.

YIELD: ONE 10-INCH BUNDT

MAKE THE MONKEY BUBBLE BREAD

Generously spray the inside of a 10-inch Bundt pan with nonstick cooking spray.

In a small saucepan, warm your milk to slightly above room temperature, then remove it from the heat, add the yeast, and whisk to dissolve. (Do not warm it beyond 110 degrees F or you will kill the yeast).

In the bowl of a standing mixer fitted with the paddle attachment, beat the flour, sugar, and salt until combined.

In a small bowl, beat the egg with a fork and add it to the dry ingredients. Mix on low speed until combined.

Keeping the mixer on low, slowly stream in the milk until combined. Add the melted butter and mix until the dough comes together. Replace the paddle attachment with the dough hook attachment. Continue to mix on medium speed until the dough becomes silky and tacky, but not sticky, 8 to 10 minutes. The dough should mound together and easily come off the bottom of the mixing bowl. (If the dough is too wet, add some flour. If it is too dry, add a tiny bit of water.)

Ingredients

FOR THE MONKEY BUBBLE BREAD

1¼ cups whole milk

2 teaspoons instant yeast

4 cups all-purpose flour

5 tablespoons sugar

1 teaspoon salt

1 egg

5 tablespoons unsalted butter, melted

FOR THE CINNAMON SUGAR COATING

1¼ cups firmly packed dark brown sugar

2 teaspoons cinnamon

½ cup (1 stick) unsalted butter, melted and cooled

Baked Note

There are a lot of monkey bread misconceptions, and I will do my darnedest to dispel them. First, you do not need an icing or topping for this bread—too sweet. Second, you can make the dough ahead of time. Once the dipped dough has been placed in the pan, wrap it tightly, refrigerate it, and bring it back to room temperature to "proof" the dough before baking. Lastly, this is one of those breads that exists to be eaten warm, straight from the oven. Once the caramel begins to cool, reheat the bread in the oven before serving.

Spray the bottom and sides of a large bowl with cooking spray. Place the dough in the bowl and roll it around to make sure it is completely covered in oil. Cover the bowl with plastic wrap or a dish towel and let it rest in a warm area until the dough has doubled in size, approximately 1 hour.

Line a sheet pan with parchment paper.

Use your clean hands to push down and deflate the dough. Remove it from the bowl and pat it into a rough circle approximately 8 inches diameter. Use a bench knife or serrated knife to cut dough into 1- to 1½-inch pieces (about ½ ounce each)—alternatively, use your hands to pinch apart the dough. Roll the pieces into balls (they don't have to be perfectly round). Place the balls on the sheet pan (you will get about 60 pieces in all). Cover the balls lightly with plastic wrap.

MAKE THE CINNAMON SUGAR COATING

In a small bowl, stir together the sugar and cinnamon. Place the melted butter in a separate bowl.

ASSEMBLE THE BREAD

Remove the plastic wrap from the dough balls and dip one ball in the melted butter. Let the excess butter drip back into the bowl, roll the ball in the brown sugar mixture, and place it in the Bundt pan. Continue this process with each ball, until you have several layers, arranging them as if you are building a brick wall.

Wrap the Bundt pan tightly in plastic wrap. Set it in a warm area of the house for about 1 hour, or until the dough balls have doubled in size and appear puffy.

Preheat the oven to 350 degrees F. Remove the plastic and bake the Bundt until the top layer is deep brown and the caramel coating begins to bubble around the edges, about 30 minutes.

Cool the bread for 5 minutes, then turn it out directly onto a platter and serve warm. Should you have any leftovers (this is rare, I promise you), simply reheat them in a 300-degree oven until warm to the touch.

PUMPKIN CHEDDAR MUFFINS

IF THERE WERE A PLACE ON EARTH WHERE YOU COULD EXPERIENCE A NEW ENGLAND FALL FOR TEN MONTHS OUT OF THE YEAR, I WOULD PROBABLY MOVE THERE. I would pursue leaf peeping like a sport, build a crackling fire nightly, and indulge in every hearty autumn recipe at my whim. Until I find this utopia, I will make do with my annual three months of fall. I will churn through umpteen pumpkins (pumpkin bread, pumpkin soup, toasted pumpkin seeds) and hundreds of pounds of Vermont cheddar (grilled cheese, cheese and crackers, fondue), and on a few mornings, I will combine the two in this very autumnal muffin. Like all good muffins, this one is quick to put together. The pumpkin base is moist but spiced with cayenne and black pepper so the sharpness of the cheddar has a chance to shine. I also like to top the muffin with a little extra cheese, so you get a savory-sweet morning experience.

YIELD: 12 MUFFINS

Preheat the oven to 400 degrees F. Lightly spray each cup of a standard 12-cup muffin pan with a little bit of vegetable spray and use a paper towel to spread the oil evenly along the bottom and up the sides of each cup.

In a large bowl, whisk together the pumpkin and sour cream. Add the eggs and butter and whisk until combined.

In another large bowl, whisk together the flour, baking powder, cayenne pepper, salt, black pepper, and brown sugar. Make a well in the middle of the dry ingredients. Pour the wet ingredients into the well, and fold until just combined. Fold in three-quarters of the cheese.

Divide the batter among the muffin cups. Sprinkle the remaining cheddar and the pumpkin seeds on top of the muffins. Bake them for 20 minutes, or until golden brown. Let the muffin pan cool on a rack for 10 minutes before turning out the muffins. Serve them warm.

Muffins taste best when eaten fresh, but they can be made ahead of time and reheated in a 200-degree oven.

Ingredients

1 cup canned solid-pack pumpkin puree

3 tablespoons sour cream

2 large eggs

½ cup (1 stick) unsalted butter, melted and cooled

2 cups all-purpose flour

1½ teaspoons baking powder

¼ teaspoon cayenne pepper

1½ teaspoons salt

1½ teaspoons freshly ground black pepper

½ cup firmly packed dark brown sugar

1¼ cups (about 4 ounces) grated sharp cheddar

2 tablespoons pumpkin seeds, optional

Baked Note

I am addicted to the raw-milk cheddar offered by several farms in Vermont. The flavors are more dimensional than ordinary cheddar (though, yes, I am still a fan of the pasteurized version); raw-milk cheeses are nutty and chocolatey and earthy—and different from farm to farm. This recipe works well with any cheddar, the sharper the better, but make sure you try a raw-milk one if the opportunity presents itself (in or out of this muffin recipe).

FOR THE DOUGHNUTS

3½ cups all-purpose flour

¾ cup granulated sugar

½ teaspoon baking soda

2 teaspoons baking powder

1 teaspoon salt

1 teaspoon freshly grated nutmeg

1 teaspoon cinnamon

2 large eggs

¾ cup buttermilk

¼ cup sour cream

¼ cup (½ stick) unsalted butter, melted
and slightly browned and cooled

Vegetable oil for frying

FOR THE CHOCOLATE DIP

4 ounces good-quality dark chocolate (60
to 70%), coarsely chopped

½ cup heavy cream

2 tablespoons unsalted butter

Sprinkles to decorate (optional)

FOR THE VANILLA GLAZE

2 cups confectioners' sugar

¼ cup whole milk

1 teaspoon vanilla paste or 1½ teaspoons
pure vanilla extract

Sprinkles to decorate (optional)

FOR THE CINNAMON SUGAR

1¼ cups granulated sugar

3 tablespoons cinnamon

FARM STAND BUTTERMILK DOUGHNUTS THREE WAYS

IF I WERE A BETTER PERSON, I WOULD MAKE THESE MORE OFTEN. I would avoid the supermarket or mass-produced doughnut. I would take a stand and refuse to eat a doughnut that was not prepared by hand and eaten fresh from the fryer. These delicious doughnuts are what a doughnut should be, the type you might pick up from the side of the road at a local farm or farm stand. And though I'm often too lazy and lethargic to fire up the fryer, they really aren't that difficult to make.

Farm stand doughnuts are usually sold coated with cinnamon sugar and tucked inside a paper bag. Sometimes they are made with cider, and sometimes they are made with buttermilk, and they are always worth stopping for. I prefer the buttermilk variety (it produces a cakier doughnut), and I prefer mine dipped in chocolate, but they taste great au naturel as well.

Each topping makes enough for one batch of doughnuts. If you want to use more than one topping for your batch, reduce the amounts by half or by two-thirds, accordingly.

YIELD: ABOUT 10 LARGE DOUGHNUTS PLUS DOUGHNUT HOLES

MAKE THE DOUGHNUTS

Line one baking sheet with parchment paper and another baking sheet with two layers of paper towels.

In a large bowl, whisk together the flour, sugar, baking soda, baking powder, salt, nutmeg, and cinnamon.

In a medium bowl, whisk the eggs, buttermilk, and sour cream until combined. Add the melted, cooled butter and whisk again.

Make a well in the center of the flour mixture and pour the liquid ingredients into the well. With a rubber spatula, slowly fold the flour into the liquid center until the mixture forms a sticky dough.

Turn the dough out onto a work surface lightly dusted with flour. Sprinkle the top of the dough with flour and pat it out until it is about ½ inch thick.

Use two round cutters (3¼ inch and 1½ inch for large doughnuts; 2½ inch and 1 inch for smaller doughnuts). Dip the large cutter in flour and press out the rounds. Dip the smaller cutter in the flour and cut out the center of each dough round. Arrange both doughnuts and doughnut holes on the parchment-lined baking sheet, pat the dough scraps back together, and use them to make as many more doughnuts and doughnut holes as possible. Chill the dough while you heat the oil.

Pour enough oil into a deep skillet to make a layer approximately 1 inch to 1½ inches deep. Slowly heat the oil over medium-high heat until it is 365 to 370 degrees F.

While you are waiting for the oil to reach temperature, make the assorted toppings.

MAKE THE CHOCOLATE DIP

Place the chopped chocolate in a medium wide-mouthed bowl. In a small saucepan, heat the cream until it is just about to boil. Pour the cream over the chocolate and wait 1 minute. Whisk until smooth. Whisk in the butter. Keep the mixture warm.

MAKE THE VANILLA GLAZE

In a medium wide-mouthed bowl, whisk together the sugar, the milk, and the vanilla paste.

MAKE THE CINNAMON SUGAR

In a medium wide-mouthed bowl, whisk together the sugar and cinnamon.

TO FRY THE DOUGHNUTS

Once the oil reaches temperature, gently lift the large doughnuts off the baking sheet and place them in the hot oil. Do not crowd the skillet—make no more than 3 doughnuts at a time. Once they have browned on one side (this takes 2 to 3 minutes), turn them over with tongs or a slotted spoon and continue to cook for another minute or just until browned (they can overcook or burn rather quickly). Using a slotted spoon, transfer the doughnuts to the paper towel–lined baking sheet and continue to fry the rest of the dough until finished. The doughnut holes will cook faster and can be made in two or three batches after the doughnuts are done.

ASSEMBLE THE DOUGHNUTS

Once you have finished frying, work quickly to dip the doughnuts in the chocolate or vanilla glaze, or the cinnamon sugar. If you like, decorate the chocolate or vanilla doughnuts with sprinkles. Serve immediately.

Ingredients

2 cups unbleached all-purpose flour

¼ cup granulated sugar

¼ cup dark unsweetened cocoa powder
(like Valrhona)

1 tablespoon baking powder

½ teaspoon salt

6 tablespoons (¾ stick) cold unsalted
butter, cut into chunks

1 large egg

½ cup heavy cream

¾ cup toasted hazelnuts, coarsely chopped

½ cup Nutella

Baked Note

My number-one piece of advice for those
new to scone making: Do not knead too
much. I think we must be born with an
urge to create perfect, smooth, pliable,
pillowy dough. Resist the temptation. Stop
working the dough the minute it comes
together. Do not worry if there are a few
dry bits scattered throughout.

NUTELLA SCONES

YES, RENATO AND I LOVE NUTELLA, THE LITTLE (OR BIG) JAR OF HAZELNUT AND CHOCOLATE
BLISS FROM ITALY. Once stocked only by specialty stores, Nutella can now be
found virtually everywhere. If you have not tried it, I beg you to stop everything, go to the nearest grocery store, and buy at least two jars: one for baking
and one for a daily midday boost directly from said jar to your mouth.

These scones (secretly my favorite scones) have a decent-size dollop of
Nutella folded into a cocoa-based dough. They aren't overly sweet, and the
hazelnuts provide a great texture. Technically, they are still a breakfast treat,
but they tend to make a bigger splash at brunch when people feel better about
eating indulgently. Scones, no matter the ingredients, are still technically
more difficult to put together than a muffin or quick bread. They require a
little practice to perfect (i.e., getting a feel for the texture you want as you
work in the butter and making sure you don't overwork the dough). However, once you master the scone, it will take you just a few moments to put
together, bake, and serve a comfy little breakfast or tea snack. If you prefer
to make your own, all-natural "Nutella," see the Homemade Nutella recipe
on page 198.

YIELD: 6 TO 8 SCONES

Preheat the oven to 375 degrees F and place the rack in the center. Line a baking sheet with parchment paper.

In a large bowl, whisk the flour, sugar, cocoa powder, baking powder, and salt
until combined.

Add the butter. Use your fingertips to rub it into the flour until the butter is
pea size and the mixture is coarse.

In a separate bowl, whisk together the egg and cream. Slowly pour the wet
ingredients into the dry ingredients and stir until the dough just comes
together. Gently and briefly knead the dough with your hands. Add the
toasted hazelnuts and knead gently to incorporate. Flatten the dough into
a rectangle approximately 6 by 12 inches (it does not need to be precise) and
spread ¼ cup of the Nutella on top in a crisscross pattern. Roll the dough up
to make a cylinder about 6 inches long, turn it on its end, and gently flatten it
into a disk about 1¾ inches high. Do not overwork the dough.

Cut the dough into 6 or 8 wedges and place them on the prepared baking sheet. Bake the scones for 18 to 20 minutes, rotating the baking sheet halfway through, or until a toothpick inserted into the center of a scone comes out clean. Do not overbake.

Transfer the scones to a wire rack to cool completely. Place the baking sheet with the parchment still on it underneath the rack.

ASSEMBLE THE NUTELLA SCONES

Heat the remaining ¼ cup Nutella in a microwave until pourable, about 10 seconds on high. Pierce the tops of the scones a few times with a fork. Use a spoon (or two spoons—one to scoop, one to scrape) to drip the warm Nutella in a zigzag pattern over the tops of the hot scones. Transfer them to a refrigerator to set for 5 minutes, then serve immediately.

Most scones have a lifespan of 24 hours or less; however, these scones taste pretty darn good on day two provided you wrap them tightly and store them at room temperature.

CARROT COCONUT SCONES
WITH CITRUS GLAZE

CARROTS HAVE LONG BELONGED TO THE SWEET BAKING SPECTRUM. In fact, it is likely that cakes sweetened with carrot have been around for many centuries and that carrot cake–type recipes like those we are familiar with today started appearing as early as 1914. Carrots have a high sugar content and subtle taste, which makes them easy to sneak into all manner of baked goods. Additionally, I have succumbed to deep self-delusion and equate all carrot baked things with health and nutrition. True, carrots contain vast amounts of vitamin A and dietary fiber, but a scone is still a scone (and for that matter, a cake is still a cake). These carrot scones are delectable whatever their nutritional value. (Like all scones, they are at their very best the day they are made.) They are dense without being heavy, sweet without being cloying, and the coconut adds some simple texture.

YIELD: 6 TO 8 SCONES

MAKE THE CARROT COCONUT SCONES

Preheat the oven to 400 degrees F and position the rack in the center. Line a baking sheet with parchment paper.

In a large bowl, whisk together the flour, sugar, oats, baking powder, salt, and shredded sweetened coconut.

Add the butter. Use your fingertips to rub the butter into the flour until the butter is pea size and the mixture is coarse.

In a separate bowl, whisk together the egg, buttermilk, vanilla and carrot puree. Slowly pour the wet ingredients into the dry ingredients and stir until the dough just comes together. Gently and briefly knead the dough with your hands. The dough will be sticky and may need to be sprinkled with flour.

Roll the dough up, turn it on its end, and gently flatten it into a disk about 1¾ inches high. Do not overwork the dough.

Whisk the egg white with 1 tablespoon water. Set aside.

Ingredients

FOR THE SCONES

2¾ cups all-purpose flour

½ cup granulated sugar

½ cup rolled oats

1 tablespoon baking powder

¼ teaspoon salt

1 cup shredded sweetened coconut

½ cup (1 stick) cold unsalted butter, cut into ½-inch chunks

1 large egg

¾ cup buttermilk

1 tablespoon pure vanilla extract

¼ cup carrot puree

1 egg white, beaten

FOR THE CITRUS GLAZE

1 tablespoon fresh lemon juice

2 tablespoons fresh orange juice

1 cup confectioners' sugar

Baked Note

I can assume that if you are attempting this recipe, you are not expecting a classic English scone. I feel obliged to tell everyone that this is more of a "morning cookie" with a scone ego. Make no mistake—this scone is less sweet than a typical cookie, and the oats and carrot lend an air of nutrition, but deep down this is a perfect treat for morning, noon, and night. Queen Elizabeth might scoff, but no one else will.

Cut the dough into 6 or 8 wedges and place the scones on the prepared baking sheet. Brush the tops with the egg white wash. Bake for 18 to 20 minutes, rotating the baking sheet halfway through, or until a toothpick inserted into the center of a scone comes out clean. Do not overbake.

Transfer the scones to a wire rack to cool completely. Place the baking sheet, with the parchment still on it, underneath the rack.

MAKE THE CITRUS GLAZE

Whisk all ingredients together in a medium bowl. The glaze should be loose enough to drizzle. If it is too thick, add a little more orange juice. If it is too loose, add a little more confectioners' sugar.

Drizzle the glaze over the scones and allow it to set before serving.

QUICK CARROT PUREE

Truthfully, I prefer carrots in the "puree" form. I prefer carrot soup to carrot sticks and a carrot–mashed potato concoction to a side of steamed carrots. I use this puree in various recipes (cakes, pancakes, lasagna, and soup), and it is quick, easy, and perfect for our Carrot Coconut Scones. Double it, triple it, and freeze for later use.

1 medium carrot
¼ cup orange juice

Place the carrot and orange juice in a medium glass microwaveable bowl. Cover or wrap tightly in plastic wrap.

Microwave on high for about 5 minutes. If the carrot is fork-tender, it is ready. If it is not fork-tender, continue to microwave in 30-second bursts until it is.

Blend (in blender or food processor) the carrot and the orange juice until smooth or, alternatively, mash with a potato masher until lump free.

BAKED CHEESE GRITS

I HAD TO SNEAK THIS SAVORY RECIPE INTO THE BOOK. Though, thematically, it is quite different from everything else in this book, grits—specifically these baked cheese grits—make up a large portion of my cooking and baking DNA. I was first introduced to grits—real stone-ground grits swimming in butter and cheese—while nursing a fairly nasty hangover during my first year of college at the University of Alabama, Tuscaloosa. It was the beginning of a beautiful relationship that has outlasted many others. Grits, a staple of Southern cuisine, are as homey, comfortable, variable, and delicious as America's beloved macaroni and cheese. I hope everyone will have a chance to try this neglected delicacy, as it is more than just a Southern caricature and maligned stereotype. Honestly, grits in any form please me. They are wonderful without adornment, and even better with copious amounts of butter and cheese. This basic recipe for baked cheese grits (adapted from *The Lee Bros. Southern Cookbook*) is a breakfast crowd-pleaser and the perfect accompaniment to bacon or sausages.

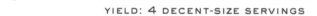

YIELD: 4 DECENT-SIZE SERVINGS

Lightly butter the bottom and sides of a 10-inch cast-iron skillet or, alternatively, a similar size baking dish.

Pour the milk and 2 cups water into a medium saucepan, cover, and heat on medium-high until the mixture boils, about 5 minutes. Uncover the pot, add the grits, salt, and pepper, and reduce the heat to medium. Stir constantly until grits are the consistency of thick soup, about 8 minutes. Reduce to a simmer, stirring every 2 minutes, and cook for about 15 to 20 minutes to let the grits thicken further. Cook for 10 to 15 minutes longer, stirring constantly to prevent the grits from sticking to the bottom of the pan. The grits will be really thick at this point.

Remove the pan from the heat and stir in ¾ cup of the cheddar cheese, ¾ cup of the Monterey Jack cheese, and the butter. Pour the grits into the prepared skillet and top them with the remaining cheeses. Turn the oven to broil.

Place the skillet directly under the heating element for 2 to 3 minutes, or until the cheese topping is melted and starts to brown. Serve immediately.

Ingredients

2 cups whole milk

1 cup stone-ground grits

1 teaspoon kosher salt

1 teaspoon freshly ground black pepper

1 cup, packed, grated extra-sharp cheddar cheese, about 4 ounces

1 cup, packed, grated Monterey Jack cheese, about 4 ounces

1 tablespoon unsalted butter

Baked Note

What is the difference between stone-ground and instant grits? Well, technically, instant grits are grits with the germ (i.e., the healthy part) removed. Tastewise, I liken instant grits to instant mashed potatoes: flavorless, manufactured, and without depth. I may be terribly lazy in the kitchen, and you won't find me making my own peanut butter anytime soon, but I beg of you, always use stone-ground grits.

MOM'S OLIVE OIL ORANGE BUNDT

TECHNICALLY SPEAKING, THIS LIGHT AND PLEASING ORANGE CAKE IS NOT RENATO'S MOM'S. Renato's mom would be the first to admit this. It belonged to his mother's neighbor, a lovely French woman named Annette, who arrived and left their neighborhood in Queens before he was born. So, yes, this is really Annette's Olive Oil Orange Bundt (Annette from Marseille, France, to give proper attribution), but his mom adapted and baked it so many times, he truly associates it only with her. Mom's Olive Oil Orange Bundt is great for breakfast with tea and coffee, or sliced and served in the afternoon with a tart dessert wine.

YIELD: ONE 10-INCH BUNDT

Preheat the oven to 350 degrees F. Generously spray the inside of a 10-inch Bundt pan with nonstick cooking spray; alternatively, butter it well, dust it with flour, and knock out the excess flour.

In a large bowl, whisk together the flour, baking powder, and salt. Set aside.

In the bowl of a standing mixer fitted with the paddle attachment, beat the egg yolks until they are pale and light; slowly pour in the sugar until it is completely incorporated. Add the yogurt and olive oil and mix until thoroughly combined. Add the orange zest and vanilla, and mix until just incorporated.

Add the flour mixture to the wet ingredients in two parts, beating after each addition until just combined (this will take about 10 seconds). Scrape down the bowl and beat again for 5 seconds.

In another large bowl, beat the egg whites until stiff peaks form. Scoop 1 cup of the egg whites into the batter. Use a rubber spatula to gently fold them in. After about 30 seconds of folding, add the remaining egg whites and gently fold until they are almost completely combined. Do not rush the folding process.

Pour the batter into the prepared pan and bake for 40 to 50 minutes, rotating the pan halfway through the baking time, or until a small sharp knife inserted into the cake comes out clean. Transfer the pan to a wire rack to cool com-

pletely. Gently loosen the sides of the cake from the pan (I sometimes use an offset spatula for this) and turn it out onto the rack.

Just before serving, dust the cake with the confectioners' sugar.

The cake can be stored at room temperature, covered tightly, for up to 3 days.

 ## TO GLAZE OR NOT TO GLAZE

Throughout Renato's entire childhood, he enjoyed this cake sans glaze. I can only assume that his mom thought a glaze was unnecessary and too sweet. However, I will admit that this quick-and-easy orange glaze makes a great visual and is a great way to use up the oranges you zested for the cake.

2 cups confectioners' sugar
¼ cup fresh orange juice

In a large bowl, whisk together the confectioners' sugar and orange juice until the glaze is pourable. (If it is too thick, add a few more drops of orange juice. If it is too thin, add a few more tablespoons of confectioners' sugar.) Drizzle the glaze along the crown of the Bundt, allowing it to drip down the sides. Allow the glaze to set before serving.

OATMEAL CHOCOLATE CHIP CAKE WITH CREAM CHEESE FROSTING

IT MAY SOUND DEVILISH, BUT THIS CAKE—WHICH IS LIKE A DENSE BANANA BREAD WITH THE FLAVOR OF A REALLY GOOD OATMEAL CHOCOLATE CHIP COOKIE—IS PERFECT FOR BREAKFAST. It is like coffee cake for the cookie enthusiast. Of course, it is also ideal for either an afternoon or a midnight snack, but it was conceived as a breakfast treat. The original recipe was buried deep within a Time-Life cookbook, and it revealed a split personality: Half the cake felt like an ambrosia, while the other half felt like a fancy coffee-klatch dessert. It was the South (ambrosia) meets North (coffee klatch) aspect of the dessert that originally caught my eye, and I have been making it ever since. Though I am hesitant to mention it, the delicious cream cheese frosting is not necessary if you are attempting a strict coffee cake interpretation. If you are serving it as an afternoon snack, however, the frosting adds a sweet little sugar rush.

YIELD: ONE 9-BY-13-INCH CAKE

MAKE THE CAKE

Preheat the oven to 375 degrees F and position the rack in the center. Butter the sides and bottom of a 9-by-13-inch glass or light-colored metal baking pan. Heat 1¼ cups water to boiling.

Place the chocolate chips in a small bowl and toss them with the bourbon until covered. Sprinkle 2 tablespoons of the flour over the chips and toss until coated. This will keep them from settling at the bottom during baking. Set aside.

Place the oats and cubed butter in a large bowl. Pour the boiling water over the oat mixture, wait 30 seconds, and stir to moisten all the oats and melt the butter. Set the mixture aside for 25 to 30 minutes.

In a separate bowl, whisk together the eggs, both sugars, salt, baking soda, baking powder, and cinnamon until combined. Fold in the cooled oatmeal and stir until well combined. Gently fold in the remaining flour and then the chocolate chips. Pour the batter into the prepared pan.

Ingredients

FOR THE CAKE

8 ounces chocolate chips

½ teaspoon bourbon, Scotch, or favorite liquor

1½ cups plus 2 tablespoons all-purpose flour

1 cup rolled oats

½ cup (1 stick) unsalted butter, cut into small cubes, at room temperature

2 eggs, slightly beaten

¾ cup granulated sugar

1¼ cups firmly packed dark brown sugar

½ teaspoon salt

1 teaspoon baking soda

1 teaspoon baking powder

1½ teaspoons cinnamon

FOR THE CREAM CHEESE FROSTING

5 tablespoons unsalted butter, softened

5½ ounces cream cheese, softened

2 cups confectioners' sugar, sifted

¾ teaspoon pure vanilla extract

Baked Note

Unlike most of my favorite cakes, this one does not require a standing mixer. You do not have to cream any butter or whip any egg whites. You just dump in the ingredients, stir, and fold. It is quick, easy, and satisfying. The cake tastes great right out of the oven, but most of my tasters and testers think it's best after resting for a day.

Bake the cake for 40 to 45 minutes, or until a toothpick inserted in the center comes out clean.

Let the cake cool in the pan on a wire rack for at least 30 minutes.

MAKE THE CREAM CHEESE FROSTING

In the bowl of a standing mixer fitted with the paddle attachment, beat the butter until it is completely smooth. Add the cream cheese and beat until combined.

Add the confectioners' sugar and vanilla and beat until smooth, about 1 minute. Cover the bowl tightly and refrigerate for at least 30 minutes. (The frosting can be made 1 day ahead. Let it soften at room temperature before using.)

ASSEMBLE THE CAKE

Spread a thin, even layer of frosting over the cooled cake. Chill it for 15 minutes so that it can set. Slice and serve. The frosted cake can be kept, refrigerated and tightly covered, for up to 3 days. Bring the cake back to room temperature before serving. (An unfrosted one will keep for 3 days, tightly covered, at room temperature.)

HONEY CORN MUFFINS

THIS MUFFIN MOMENT BEGAN FOR RENATO WITH A BOX OF BASIC JIFFY-BRAND CORN MUFFIN MIX. The boxed mix, ever present in his college apartment, produces a simple and straightforward muffin. It is not revelatory. It is sturdy and sound. However, Renato also found that it is extremely versatile as a base recipe, and he set about playing with new additions to zest up the Jiffy muffin. He tried chipotle for a little smoky heat, canned corn for texture, and honey for sweetness. The honey corn muffin was the clear favorite, and he eventually conceived of a recipe that didn't rely on the boxed mix. The honey adds a hint of sweetness without being overt, and the muffin is light (some would say more Northern in origin) without losing any character. Serve these warm and with lashings of butter and more honey.

YIELD: 12 MUFFINS

Preheat the oven to 400 degrees F. Lightly spray each cup of a standard 12-cup muffin pan with a little bit of vegetable spray and use a paper towel to spread the oil evenly along the bottom and up the sides of each cup.

In a medium bowl, lightly whisk the eggs. Add the buttermilk, honey, and butter and whisk again until combined. Set aside.

In a large bowl, whisk together the cornmeal, flour, baking powder, both sugars, and salt. Make a well in the middle of the dry ingredients, pour the wet ingredients into the well, and fold the dry into the wet until just mixed.

Fill each muffin cup about three-quarters full. Tap the bottom of the pan against counter to level the batter. Bake for 12 to 15 minutes, or until the tops are golden brown and a toothpick inserted in the center of a muffin comes out clean. Transfer the pan to a wire rack to cool for 10 to 15 minutes. Pop the muffins out while they're still warm and serve them with a generous helping of butter or honey.

Leftover muffins (should you have any) taste great sliced and toasted in a toaster oven.

Ingredients

2 large eggs

1 cup buttermilk

¼ cup honey

¼ cup (½ stick) unsalted butter, melted and cooled

1¼ cups yellow cornmeal

¾ cup all-purpose flour

1 tablespoon baking powder

¼ cup firmly packed light brown sugar

2 tablespoons granulated sugar

1 teaspoon salt

Butter or honey to taste (for serving)

Baked Note

I have spent my entire recipe-writing career advising people to avoid dark-colored baking pans. However, this is a recipe that is improved by baking it in a heavy, dark metal muffin or cupcake tin. The pan will "brown up" the edges and the sides of your muffins perfectly, leaving a tender crumb inside. If you don't have a dark pan, no worries—they will still taste delicious.

NEW YORK-STYLE CRUMB CAKE

I LEARNED THE HARD WAY: NEW YORK-STYLE CRUMB CAKE IS NOT TO BE CONFUSED WITH COFFEE CAKE—EVER. A very passionate born and bred New Yorker (aka Renato Poliafito) informed me, quite brutally, about the not-so-subtle differences between the two. It was a dressing down I won't ever forget. It was as if I'd confused Picasso with Norman Rockwell. First and foremost, New York crumb cake is all about the crumb topping. It is obscenely large in proportion to the cake. In fact, the topping is nearly identical in thickness to—or even thicker than—the cake. Second of all, the crumb should never contain nuts—no crushed nuts, no whole nuts, no hint of a nut whatsoever. Finally, a true New York crumb cake is swirl free. This was the hardest part for me to reconcile, as I love a chocolate nut swirl, and this cake seems like a natural swirl candidate. But I obeyed the New York Crumb Commandments and am now a convert myself.

YIELD: ONE 9-BY-13-INCH CAKE

Preheat the oven to 350 degrees F and position the rack in the center. Butter the sides and bottom of a glass 9-by-13-inch pan. You can use a metal pan, but the edges of the cake may turn crispy (although that is not traditional, it is not an altogether bad thing).

MAKE THE CRUMB TOPPING

In a medium bowl, stir together both sugars, the salt, and cinnamon. Add the melted butter and whisk until combined. Fold in the flour until it is absorbed and set the mixture aside.

MAKE THE CAKE

Sift the flour, baking powder, baking soda, and salt together in a medium bowl. Set aside.

In the bowl of a standing mixer fitted with the paddle attachment, cream the butter until it is completely smooth and ribbonlike. Scrape down the bowl and add the sugar. Beat the mixture until it starts to look fluffy.

Ingredients

FOR THE CRUMB TOPPING
1 cup firmly packed dark brown sugar

½ cup granulated sugar

½ teaspoon salt

1½ tablespoons cinnamon

1 cup (2 sticks) unsalted butter, melted and warm

2½ cups all-purpose flour

FOR THE CAKE
2½ cups all-purpose flour

¾ teaspoon baking powder

1 teaspoon baking soda

½ teaspoon salt

12 tablespoons (1½ sticks) unsalted butter

1½ cups granulated sugar

2 large eggs

1¼ cups sour cream

1 teaspoon pure vanilla extract

Baked Note

Renato likes this cake with really huge crumb chunks. To attain these gargantuan boulders of sugar, make sure you give the crumb time to rest. I sometimes cheat the process and spread the topping mixture on a parchment-lined baking sheet to make it dry a bit faster; however, you don't want it to dry out completely.

Add the eggs, one at a time, and beat until incorporated. Scrape down the sides of the bowl and mix again for 30 seconds. Add the sour cream and vanilla and beat just until incorporated. Add the dry ingredients in three parts, scraping down the bowl before each addition, beating only until it is just incorporated.

ASSEMBLE THE CAKE

Pour the batter into the prepared pan. Use your hands to scoop up a handful of the topping and make a fist. The topping should hold together. Break off in chunks and drop them over the cake. Repeat to use all the topping. Remember, the topping layer will look outrageously thick.

Bake the cake for 45 to 55 minutes, or until a toothpick inserted in the middle comes out clean. Rotate the pan two times during the baking process. Cool the entire pan on a wire rack for about 30 minutes before serving.

The cake will last for 3 days, tightly covered, at room temperature.

CORNMEAL GRIDDLE CAKES

THE CORNMEAL GRIDDLE CAKE IS A HERITAGE RECIPE SO STEEPED IN NOSTALGIA THAT MANY PEOPLE ASSUME IT IS A CREATION OF THEIR FAMILY OR SMALL TOWN, BUT LIKE SO MANY OLD-SCHOOL RECIPES, THE ORIGINS ARE CLOUDY AT BEST. The term "griddle cake" is nearly synonymous with pancakes, flapjacks, and hotcakes. A cornmeal griddle cake is a pancake made with cornmeal, and the end result is hearty without being heavy. While I usually appreciate a good deal of maple syrup on my pancakes, I tend to load up my cornmeal cakes with heaps of fresh butter. It's like a fresh, hot, buttery, flat, crunchy corn muffin.

YIELD: 10 TO 12 LARGE OR 20 SMALL CAKES

In a medium bowl, sift together the flour, salt, baking powder, and baking soda. Set aside.

Bring 1½ cups water to a boil. Place the cornmeal in a large bowl. Stirring continuously, slowly pour the boiling water over the cornmeal. Keep stirring until the mixture has cooled to lukewarm, almost room temperature. Add the brown sugar and stir until combined.

In a medium bowl, whisk the eggs until pale yellow. Add the buttermilk and whisk until blended. Add the flour mixture, alternating with the buttermilk mixture, to the cornmeal in three parts (beginning and ending with the flour mixture), stirring after each addition until just combined. Stir in the melted butter.

Heat a skillet or griddle pan over medium-low heat.

Add 1 or 2 tablespoons butter to the skillet and make sure it coats the surface. (Note: The first cornmeal griddle cake soaks up a fair amount of the butter and generally speaking, will not be your best handiwork. However, the subsequent griddle cakes will be a thing of beauty.) Drop griddle cakes in ¼-cup batches into the skillet (they will spread—do not crowd the pan). Cook until the bottoms are medium-brown, about 3 minutes, and the tops are bubbly, then flip the griddle cakes over and cook the other side for about 2 minutes and serve immediately. Continue cooking and serving until all the batter is gone. Serve with generous amounts of sweet butter.

Ingredients

1¼ cups all-purpose flour

½ teaspoon salt

1 tablespoon baking powder

½ teaspoon baking soda

1 cup yellow cornmeal

2 tablespoons firmly packed light brown sugar

2 large eggs

1 cup buttermilk

2 tablespoons unsalted butter, melted

4 to 6 tablespoons unsalted butter for the skillet

Baked Note

Generally speaking, you can substitute white cornmeal for yellow cornmeal in most recipes, including this one. I believe that yellow cornmeal (which is made from yellow corn) has a "cornier" taste and prefer it for that reason. White cornmeal is made from white corn, obviously, and some people prefer its less aggressive corn taste.

MALTED WAFFLES

I ARRIVED VERY LATE TO THE WAFFLE PARTY. I suppose I had a difficult time justifying getting yet another piece of kitchen equipment (both in terms of cost and its occupation of precious kitchen storage space), and I figured my pancakes were so good no one would ever miss a waffle. I was wrong. Friends, fans, and acquaintances peppered me with waffle recipe suggestions. One Baked fan is purported to own at least six waffle irons (I hope his kitchen is larger than mine). I finally gave in and bought a basic and inexpensive waffle iron. It is not fancy, and it is not a vaunted piece of vintage cooking equipment, but it really does the trick.

I could eat malted waffles all day long, every day, and be quite satisfied. The sweet nuttiness of the malt powder renders the ordinary, simple waffle especially addictive. Personally, I like these waffles drizzled with a bit of melted butter and smattering of chocolate chips, but they taste great with pure maple syrup or confectioners' sugar and whipped cream. And if you don't have a waffle iron, you now know what to ask for on your approaching birthday. Or you could just borrow one from a wacky, waffle-addicted friend.

YIELD: MAKES ABOUT 10 WAFFLES

Preheat the oven to 225 degrees F. Prepare a waffle iron with cooking spray or vegetable oil per the manufacturer's instructions.

In a large bowl, whisk together the flour, malt powder, sugar, baking soda, baking powder, and salt. In a separate bowl, whisk the eggs slightly, add the buttermilk and butter, and whisk again.

Make a well in the center of the dry ingredients and pour the buttermilk mixture into it. Fold the dry ingredients into the wet ever so gently until just combined—there will be some visible lumps. Cook the waffles according to the manufacturer's instructions for your iron. Generally speaking, you will use ¼ to ½ cup batter per waffle (depending on the size of your waffle iron). Cook the waffles until they are golden brown or a little darker (I actually prefer darker ones). Transfer the waffles directly to a rack in your oven to keep them warm while you make the rest. Serve immediately with maple syrup, butter, and chocolate chips.

Ingredients

FOR THE BAKED FRENCH TOAST

1 loaf French, Italian or Challah
bread, about 11 ounces

5 large eggs

1 cup half-and-half

½ cup whole milk

1 teaspoon pure vanilla extract

¼ teaspoon cinnamon

½ cup whole skinned almonds,
coarsely chopped

FOR THE RASPBERRY SAUCE

1 cup fresh raspberries

2 tablespoons sugar

1 teaspoon fresh lemon juice or raspberry
liqueur

Baked Note

If you are interested in a creamier bread
pudding—type recipe, increase the half-
and-half to 1 cup and the milk to ¾ cup.
And any hearty, crusty white bread makes
a great substitute for the baguette.

BAKED FRENCH TOAST

I WISH I COULD SAY IT IS MY DEEP LOVE OF COMFORT FOOD (MAC AND CHEESE, ALL MANNER OF GRATINS, AND BAKED CHICKEN DISHES) THAT HAS ME ENTRENCHED FIRMLY IN A CASSEROLE PHASE, BUT I FEAR IT IS JUST A GRADUAL DESCENT INTO LAZINESS. I find them much easier to serve or transport to a gathering. This baked version of French toast is emblematic of this new stage in my life. It is hearty, easy—you put it together the night before your breakfast gathering—delicious, and simple to manipulate (you can swap out fruits and nuts at will).

YIELD: ONE 8-INCH SQUARE CASSEROLE (ABOUT 4 SERVINGS)

MAKE THE BAKED FRENCH TOAST

Generously butter the sides and bottom of an 8-inch square baking pan. Cut the loaf into 1- or 1½-inch slices and arrange them in the pan.

In a large bowl, whisk the eggs just until they break up. Add the half-and-half, milk, vanilla, and cinnamon. Whisk until combined. Pour the mixture over the bread slices. Cover tightly with plastic wrap and refrigerate for at least 8 hours or overnight.

Preheat the oven to 350 degrees F. Use your fingers to flip each bread slice over, making sure to coat the entire surface in the liquid. Arrange the bread in an overlapping pattern, sprinkle it with almonds, and bake for 35 to 40 minutes, or until the French toast is golden brown and the mixture is puffy. Set the French toast aside to cool in the pan.

MAKE THE RASPBERRY SAUCE

In a small saucepan, toss the raspberries with the sugar. Cook the mixture over low heat until the berries start to break down, about 10 minutes. Strain the cooked raspberry sauce into a bowl to remove the seeds, then stir in the lemon juice.

ASSEMBLE THE FRENCH TOAST

Pour the raspberry sauce directly over the warm French toast (or serve it alongside in a gravy boat) and serve immediately. Top with whole fresh raspberries, if you have any left over.

Ingredients

FOR THE DOUBLE-CHOCOLATE LOAF

¾ cup firmly packed dark brown sugar

1 cup dark unsweetened cocoa powder, (like Valrhona), sifted

1½ cups all-purpose flour

¾ cup granulated sugar

1½ teaspoons baking soda

¾ teaspoon baking powder

1 teaspoon salt

2 large eggs

1 large egg yolk

¾ cup buttermilk

½ cup vegetable oil

1 teaspoon pure vanilla extract

8 ounces good-quality dark chocolate (60 to 72%), coarsely chopped

FOR THE CREAM CHEESE SPREAD

5 ounces cream cheese, softened

2 tablespoons creamy peanut butter

⅓ cup sugar

Baked Note

This loaf is the ultimate gift. I double (or triple) the recipe, cool the loaves completely, and remove them from the pans. To give the loaves a nifty bakery look, I like to wrap the loaves in brown parchment paper, and then wrap them in plastic and drop them off to friends along with a card.

DOUBLE-CHOCOLATE LOAF
WITH PEANUT BUTTER
CREAM CHEESE SPREAD

I HAVE BEEN TOUTING THE CHOCOLATE-AS-BREAKFAST PHILOSOPHY FOR SOME TIME NOW. I am neither a medical doctor nor a nutritionist, but I wholeheartedly believe that a few bites of chocolate throughout the day will save you from an all-out midnight binge (the kind where you devour a pint of ice cream and black out). Though this philosophy has not been tested under the supervision of a scientist, I can assure you that the Double-Chocolate Loaf is a great way to start your own experimentation. It is extremely easy to make—it is a quick bread, after all—and the chocolate flavor is intense without being too sweet. Slice and eat it plain, or toast and spread it with a bit of butter, cream cheese, or our recommended spread: Peanut Butter Cream Cheese. It is wonderful with coffee and the morning newspaper.

YIELD: ONE 9-BY-5-INCH LOAF

MAKE THE DOUBLE CHOCOLATE LOAF

Preheat the oven to 350 degrees F and position the rack in the center. Butter a 9-by-5-inch loaf pan, dust it with flour, and knock out the excess flour.

Place the brown sugar in the bowl of a standing mixer fitted with the paddle attachment. Press out any lumps with the back of a large spoon. Add the cocoa, flour, granulated sugar, baking soda, baking powder, and salt. Scrape down the sides and bottom of the bowl.

In a separate bowl, whisk the eggs and egg yolk until blended, then add the buttermilk, oil, and vanilla; whisk until combined.

Turn the mixer to low and slowly stream the wet ingredients into the dry ones, mixing just until combined. Stir in the dark chocolate chunks by hand.

Pour the batter into the prepared pan and bake for 1 hour to 1 hour and 10 minutes, or until a toothpick inserted in the center of the loaf comes out clean.

Let the cake cool in the pan for 15 minutes, then turn it out onto a wire rack to cool completely.

MAKE THE PEANUT BUTTER SPREAD

In the bowl of a standing mixer fitted with the paddle attachment, beat together the cream cheese and peanut butter until smooth. Add the sugar and beat until incorporated. (If you are not using the spread immediately, place it in a ramekin, tightly cover it in plastic wrap, and refrigerate it for up to 3 days.)

Serve the loaf plain or toasted, topped with the peanut butter spread.

The loaf will keep, in an airtight container or wrapped tightly, at room temperature for up to 3 days.

During many bouts of testing several recipes for various books and articles, I noticed something quite peculiar: loaves (or quick breads) actually look and taste better baked in a conventional home oven compared with the large convection-style ovens often found in restaurants and patisseries (mine included). The longer bake of a conventional oven coupled with the absence of a convection fan allows the loaf to bake up from the bottom, creating a perfect dome, crack, and moist crumb. The convection fan, while perfect for cookies and most cakes, often bakes the loaves a tad too quick, resulting in a shorter, tighter loaf—one that is still quite delicious, but not as impressive as those produced in a home oven.

That said, I compiled a list of a few home loaf baking tips:

1

You can double (or triple) almost any loaf recipe without fail.

2

Make sure your loaf is baked all the way through. This is important, as many loaves are tricky and appear baked from the outside (including puffy dome and crack) while remaining undercooked. If you pull your loaf out early, it will collapse in on itself, creating a "sunken" loaf.

3

Loaves freeze extremely well. Let cool entirely to room temperature and just wrap tightly in two layers of plastic wrap and one layer of aluminum foil, and freeze for up two months. Bring the loaves back to room temperature by way of your refrigerator for 8 hours, then let sit at room temperature for 4 hours before unwrapping the loaves.

4

Mix-ins (chocolate chips, fruits, nuts) are hit-and-miss with loaves, depending on the density of your batter, and may sink to the bottom during baking. Toss your mix-ins in a bit of liquor, then coat them in flour to allow the mix-ins to become suspended in the batter.

TARTS AND PIES

Pies can be heartbreaking. They are burdened with the heavy weight of all-American nostalgia. That is a lot to shoulder. A pie loaded with berries or apples or nuts or custard can be uniquely disappointing—at once soggy, oversweet, tasteless, and, yes, sad. I can think of no other dessert that has been mined so deeply to reflect a grandmotherly aura, and yet so many pies do Grandma wrong.

Pies can also be otherworldly. Transformative. A seasonal treat that celebrates and showcases local ingredients like few other recipes, sweet or savory. However, there are few shortcuts to a great pie. I have yet to meet a grocery-store pie, suffocated in shrink-wrap or a mindless see-through box, that is worth one calorie. (I am okay with store-bought, slice-and-bake cookie dough, though, which mimics the home-baked thing much better.) Frozen pie crusts might save a few minutes in the kitchen, but they are uniformly boring. You lose control over thickness and flakiness. Even more unpleasant are the premade crumb crusts available these days. Homemade versions can be pulled together in less than 5 minutes and at a substantial cost savings.

Pie makers already know all of the above. The home bakers I've met in person or through e-mail never utter the words frozen or premade. Never. That's why it was so gratifying to work on this chapter. Though I deify the classic fruit pie (flaky crust encasing a fresh fruit filling), a great many other American pie and tart recipes made their way to me that were lighthearted, easy to make, and thoroughly delicious.

Our Whiskey Pear Tart (see page 78) is a showstopper. It's a little bit boozy and a little bit serious and very, very tasty. It's classic without being stuffy. The Mississippi Mud Pie (A) (see page 69) was created to satisfy a West Coast contingent that insisted the pie must be made with coffee ice cream—Mississippi Mud Pie (B) contains no ice cream at all (see page 156). I happen to like both versions a great deal. And of course, the Peanut Butter Banana Cream Pie (see page 60) deserves a cult following. It is a pie stuffed full of all of my favorite ingredients (chocolate, peanut butter, and bananas) yet it manages to taste light, sophisticated and deviously delicious.

Ingredients

3 cups all-purpose flour

1 tablespoon sugar

1 teaspoon fine salt

1 cup (2 sticks) cold unsalted butter

Baked Note

The dough will feel and look sticky, or at least stickier than you might be used to. Don't fret. Once it firms up in the fridge, it will be perfect.

CLASSIC PIE DOUGH

THIS PIE DOUGH, OUR BASIC PIE DOUGH, IS EXACTLY THE SAME AS THE ONE FROM OUR FIRST BOOK, BAKED: NEW FRONTIERS IN BAKING. There is little need for variance on this recipe. This dough is flaky, easy to work with, and a bit more forgiving than some.

YIELD: 2 BALLS OF DOUGH, ENOUGH FOR TWO SINGLE-CRUST 9-INCH PIES OR ONE DOUBLE-CRUST PIE

In a medium bowl, whisk the flour, sugar, and salt together. In a measuring cup, stir ¾ cup water with several ice cubes until it is very cold.

Cut the cold butter into cubes and toss them in the flour mixture to coat. Put the mixture in the bowl of a food processor and pulse in short bursts until the butter pieces are the size of hazelnuts.

Pulsing in 4-second bursts, slowly drizzle the ice water into the food processor through the feed tube.

As soon as the dough comes together in a ball, stop adding water. Remove the dough from the food processor and divide it in half. Flatten each piece into a disk and wrap each disk first in parchment paper and then in plastic wrap. Refrigerate the dough until firm, about 1 hour. (The dough can be kept refrigerated for up to 3 days or frozen for up to 3 months. Thaw it in the refrigerator before proceeding with your recipe.)

BUTTERMILK PIE
(WITH A HINT OF MAPLE SYRUP)

I WOKE UP ONE DAY IN THE MIDDLE OF WINTER WITH AN URGE TO VISIT QUEBEC CITY. It was a quick, fairy-tale trip complete with crackling fireplaces, large and comfortable beds, and plenty of cheese and chocolate. I was also taken with the omnipresent maple pie. Well, perhaps I was more than taken with this dessert, since I tasted many versions as I ate my way through Quebec City. It vaguely reminded me of a too-sweet version of the buttermilk pie a friend's mom used to make. Buttermilk pie is supposedly of Texan origin, though you will not find it on many Texas menus these days. It is essentially a custard thrown into a pie shell; it comes together in mere minutes (not including the baking time). I fused my favorite aspects of Canadian maple pie with that forgotten buttermilk pie and came up with this sweet maple-infused custard hybrid.

YIELD: ONE 9-INCH PIE

Dust a work surface with a sprinkling of flour and roll the dough ball out into a 12-inch round. Transfer it to a 9-inch pie plate and carefully work it into the bottom and up the sides, folding it under and crimping the edges as you go. Wrap and freeze the crust until it is firm, about 30 minutes (it will keep this way for up to 3 months).

Preheat the oven to 325 degrees F.

In large bowl, lightly beat the eggs. Whisk in 2 tablespoons of the flour. Don't be alarmed if the mixture appears curdled after the addition of the flour—it will come back together. Add both sugars and whisk until the mixture is well combined and uniform in color. Whisk in the butter, buttermilk, and maple syrup until completely combined.

Sprinkle ½ teaspoon of the remaining flour over the unbaked pie crust. Pour the batter into the shell, sprinkle with the remaining ½ teaspoon flour, and bake for about 1 hour, or until the custard is set.

Set the pie on a wire rack to cool completely. Serve it at room temperature. Refrigerate any leftover pie, tightly covered, for up to 2 days.

Ingredients

1 ball Classic Pie Dough (page 58)

4 large eggs

2 tablespoons plus 1 teaspoon flour

¾ cup granulated sugar

¼ cup firmly packed dark brown sugar

½ cup (1 stick) unsalted butter, melted and cooled

1 cup buttermilk

¼ cup pure maple syrup

Baked Note

I should warn you ahead of time that this pie, with its pale dough and brownish filling, would not win any beauty pageants. It is not a showstopper or a centerpiece, and it almost repels attempts to gussy it up. On the other hand, if you are not desperate to impress with a visual smorgasbord, this homey little pie packs a lot of unexpected taste and texture. It is sweet and custardy and captivating. Think of it as the dessert equivalent of frogs' legs—ugly, but addictive.

FOR THE VANILLA WAFER CRUST

6 ounces vanilla wafer cookies

6 tablespoons (¾ stick) cold unsalted butter, cut into ½-inch cubes

2 tablespoons sugar

FOR THE BANANA PUDDING FILLING

⅓ cup sugar

1½ tablespoons cornstarch

⅛ teaspoon salt

1 cup heavy cream

½ cup whole milk

2 large egg yolks

1 vanilla bean

1 tablespoon unsalted butter

3 ripe bananas, peeled

2 tablespoons orange juice

FOR THE PEANUT BUTTER TOPPING

3 ounces cream cheese, softened

½ cup confectioners' sugar

1 teaspoon pure vanilla extract

⅓ cup creamy peanut butter (do not use old-fashioned or freshly ground)

⅔ cup heavy cream, chilled

ASSEMBLY

1 ripe banana, peeled (optional)

1 tablespoon orange juice (optional)

Chocolate covered peanuts (optional)

PEANUT BUTTER BANANA CREAM PIE

TRUE STORY: I WAS HAUNTED BY THE BANANA CREAM PIE. For a brief period in my life, it was all I thought about and ate. I tried many variations and made many variations, but I always found something wrong with the recipe. Too sweet. Too grainy. Too slimy. I lay awake at night rethinking the details, reworking the formula in my head.

This recipe is the culmination of all my thoughts and fever dreams, and it is now officially my favorite pie to make and eat. The crust is made with a classic vanilla wafer, which is less assertive than a traditional pie crust, and the banana pudding is light and pleasing. The whole pie is topped with a layer of smooth and dreamy peanut-butter-flavored cream cheese, which brings the dessert together. No, it is not traditional, but it is delicious. Oh, and the bananas are tossed in a bit of orange juice to keep them from turning black. Trust me, you do not want to eat black bananas.

YIELD: ONE 9-INCH PIE

Preheat the oven to 350 degrees F and position the rack in the middle.

MAKE THE VANILLA WAFER CRUST

Place the vanilla wafer cookies, butter, and sugar in a food processor. Pulse in short bursts until the mixture resembles a moist crumb. Turn the mixture out into your pie plate and press it into the bottom and up the sides. Using the back of a large spoon will help you to create an even crust.

Bake the crust until it is golden brown, 10 to 12 minutes. If it begins to puff while baking, use the back of the spoon to press it gently down. Allow the baked crust to cool completely.

MAKE THE BANANA PUDDING FILLING

In a medium saucepan, whisk together the sugar, cornstarch, and salt. Slowly, while whisking continuously, stream in the cream, then the milk. Add the egg yolks. Cut the vanilla bean in half lengthwise and, using the tip of the knife or

a small teaspoon, scrape the seeds into the saucepan. Whisk until the mixture is combined. Discard the bean.

Turn the heat to medium-high and, whisking occasionally, bring the mixture to a boil, about 5 minutes. Remove the pan from the heat, add the butter, and stir vigorously for about 2 minutes to release excess heat. Spread the warm pudding over the cooled crust and chill the pie until the filling is completely cool, about 1 hour.

After the filling has chilled, thinly slice the bananas on a diagonal. Toss the slices in the orange juice. Transfer the banana slices to a paper towel and pat them dry. Arrange them in a single layer over the pudding to cover it completely. Return the pie to the refrigerator while making the peanut butter topping.

MAKE THE PEANUT BUTTER TOPPING

In the bowl of a standing mixer fitted with the paddle attachment, beat the cream cheese and confectioners' sugar until smooth. Add the vanilla and peanut butter, and beat until just combined.

In a clean bowl of a standing mixer, use the mixer fitted with the whisk attachment and whip the cream until soft peaks form. Remove the bowl from the mixer and, with a rubber spatula, gently fold the whipped cream into the peanut butter mixture until the topping is uniform in color.

Spread the peanut butter layer evenly over the bananas on the pie. Chill for at least 3 hours or as long as 8 hours.

TO ASSEMBLE THE PIE

Just before serving, thinly slice the banana on a diagonal and toss it with the orange juice.

Arrange the banana slices around the top edge of the pie, then arrange chocolate-covered peanuts around the edges of the banana slices, if desired. Serve immediately.

The pie tastes best if eaten within 24 hours. On the rare occasion that you have leftovers, wrap the pie in plastic wrap and refrigerate it for up to 3 days.

SAWDUST PIE

I JUST ASSUMED THAT SAWDUST PIE WAS A HERITAGE RECIPE. The name implies a rugged backstory, one with humble or Depression-era beginnings. I imagined the recipe was steeped in great dustbowl prairie lore and passed down to each generation with a bit of history and a sprinkling of legend. I was completely wrong. Sawdust pie was created at Patti's 1880's Settlement Restaurant in Grand Rivers, Kentucky, sometime after 1975 (the exact date is hard to pin down) and took hold in the national conscience after a version of the recipe was published in *Bon Appétit* in May 1983. The pie is composed of graham cracker crumbs, coconut, and pecans, which, when thrown together, are supposed to resemble sawdust. The original recipe was a little too sweet. I reimagined it with a little less sugar, a tiny bit of white chocolate, and some much-needed salt. The pie is usually topped with whipped cream and banana slices, and I suggest you always serve it warm.

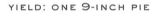

YIELD: ONE 9-INCH PIE

Dust a work surface with a sprinkling of flour. Roll out the dough ball into a 12-inch round. Transfer it to a pie dish and carefully work it into place, folding any overhang under and crimping the edge as you go. Wrap and refrigerate the crust for at least 30 minutes.

Preheat the oven to 350 degrees F.

In a large bowl, use a wooden spoon to combine the sugars, coconut, pecans, graham cracker crumbs, white chocolate, and salt. Add the egg whites and vanilla and stir until just combined—the egg whites should coat all the ingredients.

Transfer the filling to the prepared pie shell. Bake until filling is set to the touch, 30 to 40 minutes. Cool the pie for at least 1 hour before serving it warm, with whipped cream and sliced bananas, if you like.

Ingredients

1 ball Classic Pie Dough (page 58)

1 cup granulated sugar

¼ cup firmly packed dark brown sugar

1¼ cups unsweetened flaked coconut

1¼ cups pecans, coarsely chopped

1½ cups graham cracker crumbs, about 21 graham crackers

2 ounces high-quality white chocolate, coarsely chopped

½ teaspoon salt

6 egg whites

1 teaspoon pure vanilla extract

Simple Whipped Cream for serving (optional, page 159)

Sliced bananas for serving (optional)

Baked Note

I tend to add chocolate to a lot of desserts that didn't start out with it. This is simply my preference (and addiction). In a dramatic act of self-control, I did not add dark chocolate to this recipe . . . though if you share my chocolate addiction, feel free to stir in about 4 ounces of chocolate chips or chopped dark chocolate with the coconut.

ALMOND JOY TART

THOUGH I AM NOT A TRUE COCONUT PERSON, PEOPLE GO BONKERS FOR OUR COCONUT CAKES AND COCONUT MACAROONS, ESPECIALLY AT OUR CHARLESTON LOCATION, WHERE COCONUT IS KING. And I have managed to work my way into the coconut groove with this riff on the Almond Joy. That legendary candy bar was the creation of the Peter Paul Candy Manufacturing Company of Connecticut, now absorbed by Hershey's. Mr. Peter Paul Halajian certainly knew his way around coconut: He developed the Almond Joy's precursors—bars of moist coconut flake covered in chocolate—made them fresh at night, and sold them door-to-door the following day. This recipe is my wistful version of what a fresh Almond Joy must taste like.

YIELD: SIX 4-INCH INDIVIDUAL TARTS

MAKE THE ALMOND TART DOUGH

In a small bowl, lightly whisk the egg and set it aside.

Put the almonds and sugar in the bowl of a food processor and pulse until the almonds are finely ground. Add flour and salt and pulse again just until mixed. Add the butter and pulse until sandy (about 6 to 10 quick pulses). Pour in the egg and pulse just until the dough begins to cohere into a ball. Form the dough into a disk, wrap it tightly in plastic wrap, and refrigerate it for at least 1 hour or overnight.

MAKE THE COCONUT CREAM FILLING

Place the white chocolate in a medium heatproof bowl.

In a small saucepan set over medium heat, heat the cream just to a boil. Pour it over the white chocolate and let it stand for 30 seconds. Slowly, starting in the center of the bowl, whisk the cream and white chocolate until smooth. Cover and refrigerate this ganache for 4 hours or overnight before proceeding.

ASSEMBLE THE TART

Dust a work surface with flour. Place the disk of chilled dough on the work surface and divide it into 6 equal portions. Shape each into a smooth disk. (Note: The dough will be sticky. Make sure to turn it with a bench knife or

Ingredients

FOR THE ALMOND TART DOUGH

1 large egg

¼ cup whole toasted almonds

¼ cup sugar

1¼ cups plus 2 tablespoons all-purpose flour

¼ teaspoon salt

½ cup (1 stick) cold unsalted butter, cut into ½- inch cubes

FOR THE COCONUT CREAM FILLING

8 ounces good-quality white chocolate, coarsely chopped

1 cup heavy cream

2 cups unsweetened shredded coconut (if you're coconut obsessed, go ahead and use 2¼ cups)

1 tablespoon light rum

FOR THE CHOCOLATE GLAZE AND GARNISH

2 ounces good-quality milk chocolate, coarsely chopped

2 ounces good-quality dark chocolate (60 to 72%), coarsely chopped

½ cup heavy cream

6 whole toasted almonds

Baked Note

It would seem that a chocolate tart crust would be the perfect shell for a riff on the Almond Joy, but it fell short during many tests and trials. The chocolate overwhelmed the coconut, and somehow it just felt entirely contrived.

offset spatula as needed and keep the working surface floured.) Use a rolling pin to roll each piece of dough into a 5½-inch circle just over ⅛ inch thick. Very gently press each dough round into a 4-inch tart pan with removable bottom.

Place the tart pans in the freezer for 30 minutes. Preheat the oven to 375 degrees F.

Line the tart crusts with aluminum foil, and fill each one three-quarters full with pie weights or dried beans. Bake them for 15 minutes, then remove the foil and weights and bake for another 10 minutes, or until lightly browned. Transfer the tart pans to a wire rack to cool.

MAKE THE COCONUT CREAM FILLING

Meanwhile, in the bowl of a standing mixer fitted with the whisk attachment, beat the white chocolate ganache at medium speed until soft peaks form. Do not overwhip. Gently fold in the coconut and the rum. Divide the filling evenly among the cooled tart shells and place them in the refrigerator while you make the chocolate glaze.

MAKE THE CHOCOLATE GLAZE

Place the milk and dark chocolates in a medium heatproof bowl.

In a small saucepan, heat the heavy cream until it is just about to boil. Pour it over the chocolates and whisk to combine. Let the mixture set for about 10 minutes. Remove the tarts from the refrigerator and spoon the glaze evenly over each one. Top each tart with one almond and refrigerate again until the glaze sets up, about 10 minutes.

The tarts can be stored, tightly covered, in the refrigerator for up to 2 days.

PEACHES AND DREAM PIE

I SPENT A GOOD PART OF MY YOUTH IN THE MIDDLE OF FLORIDA, FLUSH AGAINST THE GULF OF MEXICO. I lived in a subdivision of a subdivision, as was the nature of the beast, and I was blissfully unaware of the farmers' market revolution stirring in other parts of the country. All our fruit was purchased from a dimly lit grocery store, and often we bought the canned variety—we viewed canned fruit as a much better nutritional alternative to, say, cookies.

This creamy peach pie is a great revision of a recipe that has floated about the country in many forms. It is tasty, as well as quick and easy to put together. On a side note, I did unearth several no-bake peaches-and-cream pie recipes... I did everyone a favor and promptly reburied them.

YIELD: ONE 9-INCH PIE

MAKE THE CRUST

Dust a work surface with a sprinkling of flour. Roll the dough ball out into a 12-inch round. Transfer the dough to a pie dish and carefully work it into place, folding any overhang under and crimping the edge as you go. Cover the crust in plastic wrap and refrigerate it for at least 30 minutes. Preheat the oven to 375 degrees F.

MAKE THE PEACHES AND DREAM FILLING

Arrange the peach halves cut side up on the bottom of the pie shell or spread the diced fresh peaches in the pie shell. In a medium bowl, whisk together the eggs, sour cream, and honey until they just come together. Sprinkle the mixture with the salt, brown sugar, and flour, and whisk until just combined. Pour the mixture over the peaches.

MAKE THE PIE TOPPING

Place the sugar, flour, and butter in a bowl. Use your hand to work the butter into the dry ingredients until the mix looks like coarse sand. Assemble the pie. Sprinkle the pie topping across the filling, and bake for 45 minutes, or until the filling is bubbly (place a sheet pan on the oven rack directly below the pie to catch any filling that bubbles over). Let the pie cool overnight before serving.

Ingredients

1 ball Classic Pie Dough (page 58)

FOR THE PEACHES AND DREAM FILLING

10 canned peach halves, or about 2½ cups fresh diced, peeled peaches

2 large eggs

1 cup sour cream

2 tablespoons honey

¼ teaspoon salt

½ cup firmly packed dark brown sugar

2 tablespoons all-purpose flour

FOR THE PIE TOPPING

½ cup firmly packed dark brown sugar

⅓ cup all-purpose flour

4 tablespoons cold unsalted butter, cut into ½-inch pieces

Baked Note

At least 90 percent of the peaches-and-cream pie recipes that crossed my path while I researched this book specified the use of canned peaches. Perhaps they were written in that era when fresh peaches were difficult to locate, or perhaps the sugar content of a canned peach was an added plus, but I tested fresh peaches in place of their canned counterparts in several recipes without any problems.

MISSISSIPPI MUD PIE (A),
AKA COFFEE ICE CREAM TART

USUALLY THE DIFFERENCES IN A POPULAR RECIPE—SAY RED VELVET CAKE—ARE A MATTER OF SUBTLE VARIATIONS (I.E., LESS FLOUR, MORE SUGAR, CREAM CHEESE FROSTING VERSUS VANILLA FROSTING) AND PERSONAL TWEAKS (SOME PEOPLE TRADE THE RED FOOD DYE FOR BEET JUICE). However, on occasion, a recipe will undergo seismic differences from state to state and person to person. The Mississippi Mud Pie is one of those recipes. Mississippi mud means many things to many people, and we took the liberty of reinterpreting two of the most popular versions (see version B on page 156). This recipe is the simpler one. In fact, you can put it together rather effortlessly (though there are stretches of time to account for the chilling and freezing steps), and I find that perfectly charming: chocolate cookie crust covered in a layer of chocolate fudge covered in a layer of coffee ice cream and drizzled with more bourbon fudge. You could swap the coffee ice cream for another flavor, but then you couldn't call it Mississippi mud.

YIELD: ONE 9-INCH PIE

MAKE THE CHOCOLATE COOKIE CRUST

In a food processor, pulverize the wafer cookies into a very fine crumb. You should have about 1½ cups. Place the crumbs into a bowl, add the sugar, and stir until combined.

Pour the melted butter over the crumbs and mix well. Transfer the crumb mixture to a 9-inch pie plate and press it into the bottom and up the sides. Use the back of a large spoon to get an even crust. Set the crust aside in the refrigerator.

MAKE THE FILLING

Place the chocolate in a large heatproof bowl.

In a medium saucepan, bring the cream, butter, and corn syrup to a simmer. Remove the mixture from the heat, pour it over the chocolate, and let sit for 1 minute. Then whisk the chocolate mixture until it is completely smooth. Whisk in the confectioners' sugar and bourbon.

Ingredients

FOR THE CHOCOLATE COOKIE CRUST

30 chocolate wafer cookies, about 6 ounces

1 tablespoon granulated sugar

6 tablespoons (¾ stick) unsalted butter, melted

FOR THE FILLING

4 ounces good-quality dark chocolate (60 to 72%)

¼ cup plus 1 tablespoon heavy cream

3 tablespoons unsalted butter

2 tablespoons light corn syrup

1 cup confectioners' sugar, sifted

1 tablespoon Kentucky bourbon

1 pint good-quality coffee ice cream

½ cup toasted pecans, coarsely chopped

FOR THE BOURBON FUDGE TOPPING

2 tablespoons heavy cream

2 tablespoons unsalted butter

1 tablespoon light corn syrup

3 ounces good-quality dark chocolate (60 to 72%)

1 teaspoon Kentucky bourbon

Baked Note

During our dessert explorations, I noticed the Mississippi mud devotees were among the more fanatical bakers. A few even suggested—no, demanded—that I print their specific ice cream brands or ice cream recipes in the book. In the end, I've decided that might be too restrictive. Use any high-quality store-bought coffee ice cream, with the shortest ingredient list possible, or make your own (page 181).

Spread the fudge evenly over the bottom of the pie crust, cover it, and refrigerate for 2 hours.

Soften the coffee ice cream by placing the container in the microwave for 10 seconds on high. Put it into a large bowl and use a rubber spatula to beat it until it is slightly malleable. Spread the ice cream over the chilled fudge filling, sprinkle it with pecans, gently pressing them into the ice cream, and freeze the pie for about 1½ hours, or until the ice cream is firm.

MAKE THE BOURBON FUDGE TOPPING

In a small saucepan over low heat, heat the cream, butter, and corn syrup together until the mixture begins to simmer. Remove the pan from the heat and add the chocolate. Whisk until the fudge is smooth—if you still have a few stray chocolate chunks, reheat the mixture over very low heat until they are completely melted. Stir in the bourbon.

Beat the fudge topping until it reaches room temperature, and pour it over the ice cream and pecan layer in a zigzag pattern. Freeze the Mississippi Mud Pie until it is set, about 20 minutes. To serve the pie, cut it with a warmed sharp knife.

The pie will keep in the freezer, tightly covered, for up to 4 days.

MALTED CRISP TART

TRUTH BE TOLD, MY SEARCH FOR TREASURED AND HERITAGE-INSPIRED TART RECIPES WAS A LITTLE BLEAK. I dug up hundreds of heirloom pie and cookie and cake recipes, but the tart recipes were extremely scarce, or incomplete, or not really tarts. Instead, I tasked pastry chef extraordinaire Melissa Fritz Walters with creating a tart that is a little bit malty and little bit crispy, and she built the tart of my candy-colored dreams. The Malted Crisp Tart is a Melissa-original, and it quickly became my favorite dessert. The brown sugar crust is a near perfect receptacle for the dense malted milk chocolate and light malted diplomat cream, and the layers of caramelized rice crispies provide an unexpected but ultimately desired crunch. The tart is definitely designed for a swanky gathering, but I have been known to eat a slice in my pajamas in front of the television.

YIELD: ONE 9-INCH TART

MAKE THE BROWN SUGAR CRUST

Lightly spray a napkin or paper towel with vegetable oil and use the napkin to apply the oil to the sides and bottom (and nooks and crannies) of the tart pan.

Place the flour, salt, malted milk powder, butter, sugar, and pure vanilla in a food processor and pulse until the mixture is crumbly.

Scoop the crumb mixture out into the prepared tart pan and use your hands to press the mixture into bottom and up the sides of the tart pan (the crust should not look too thick).

Preheat the oven to 350 degrees F.

Place the tart pan in the freezer for 20 minutes.

Remove the tart pan from the freezer, place on a baking sheet, and bake until the tart is golden brown, about 20-30 minutes.

Transfer the tart pan to a wire rack and cool completely.

Ingredients

FOR THE BROWN SUGAR CRUST

1½ cups all-purpose flour

¼ teaspoon salt

1 tablespoon malted milk powder

10 tablespoons (1¼ sticks) unsalted butter, chilled (cut into ½-inch pieces)

½ cup firmly packed light brown sugar

½ teaspoon pure vanilla extract

FOR THE CARAMELIZED CRISPIES

⅓ cup sugar

2 cups crisped rice cereal

FOR THE MILK CHOCOLATE GANACHE

8 ounces good-quality milk chocolate, coarsely chopped

⅔ cup heavy cream

2 teaspoons malted milk powder

FOR THE MALTED DIPLOMAT CREAM

1¼ cups whole milk

⅓ cup sugar

1 large egg yolk

1 large egg

1 tablespoons plus 1½ teaspoons cornstarch

2 tablespoons malted milk powder

2 tablespoons unsalted butter

2 teaspoons pure vanilla extract

5 ounces heavy cream

FOR THE TART ASSEMBLY

1 cup crushed malted milk balls

Malted Milk Balls, to garnish

Caramelized Crispies, to garnish

Baked Note

Yes, there are a lot of bowls involved in this recipe, but it is not difficult—so don't be afraid to attempt it. I tried to break out the steps in an orderly manner, but feel free to break it up over two days: make the tart dough (unbaked) and caramelized crispies on the first day and the other parts on day two.

MAKE THE CARAMELIZED CRISPIES

Line a half-sheet baking pan with a Silpat or, alternatively, a sheet of aluminum foil sprayed with vegetable oil.

In a small saucepan over low heat, stir together 2 tablespoons water with the sugar and bring just to a very low boil for about 1 minute.

Add the crisped rice cereal and stir until the mixture is dry. Keep stirring until sugar begins to caramelize and the pan begins to smoke. Fold the mixture over and over until all the crispies are coated with an amber layer of sugar. Once the crispies are completely coated, turn them out onto the Silpat and cool completely.

Break the candy up into large chunky pieces and set aside.

MAKE THE MILK CHOCOLATE GANACHE

Place the milk chocolate in a medium-size heatproof bowl.

In a small saucepan over low heat, whisk together the heavy cream and malt powder. Bring the mixture to a simmer (tiny bubbles will form around the edges of the cream; it should not be a rolling boil). Remove from the heat and pour over the milk chocolate. Let the mixture sit for 2 minutes. Starting in the center of the bowl, and working your way out to the edges, whisk the chocolate ganache in a circle until completely smooth.

TO BEGIN ASSEMBLING THE TART

Gently pour the ganache into the cooled tart shell. Top with crushed malted milk balls and 1 cup caramelized crispies. Very gently press the crushed malt balls and caramelized crispies into the ganache.

Refrigerate the tart while you make the Malted Diplomat Cream.

MAKE THE MALTED DIPLOMAT CREAM

Set a fine-mesh sieve over a medium bowl.

In a medium saucepan, bring the milk to a simmer and keep warm.

In a medium bowl, whisk the sugar, egg yolk, egg, cornstarch, and malted milk powder together until the mixture is pale, about 1 minute.

Whisk half of the warm milk into the egg yolk mixture, then pour the mixture into the remaining milk in the saucepan and cook over medium heat, whisking constantly, until thickened, about 5 minutes. Remove from the heat and whisk in the butter and vanilla. Strain the pastry cream through the sieve and press a piece of plastic wrap directly onto the surface of the cream to prevent a skin from forming. Put in the refrigerator for about 1 hour until chilled.

Remove the pastry cream from the refrigerator and whip until creamy.

In a separate bowl, whip the heavy cream with a whisk until soft peaks form and fold into the pastry cream.

FINISH ASSEMBLING THE TART

Remove the tart from the refrigerator and cover the Milk Chocolate Malt layer with the Malted Diplomat Cream. Garnish with a few whole malt balls and caramelized crispies. Refrigerate the tart to set up, about 30 minutes, and serve immediately. The tart can be stored, tightly covered, in the refrigerator for up to 2 days.

FOR THE ORANGE CREAM SODA FILLING

½ cup (1 stick) unsalted butter, cut into ½-inch cubes

1¼ teaspoons unflavored gelatin

Zest and juice of 2 medium lemons (2 tablespoons zest and ¼ cup juice)

Zest and juice of 3 large oranges (3 tablespoons zest and 1 cup juice)

1 cup orange cream soda

3 large eggs

2 large egg yolks

¾ cup sugar

FOR THE ORANGE TART DOUGH

½ cup (1 stick) unsalted butter

¼ cup sugar

Zest of 1 orange (2 tablespoons)

¼ teaspoon salt

1 large egg

1½ cups all-purpose flour

FOR THE ORANGE WHIPPED TOPPING

1 cup heavy cream

2 tablespoons sugar

2 tablespoons orange cream soda

Baked Note

If you want to add a little more sweetness to your tart (and to keep the crust from getting soggy) brush the bottom of the tart shell with 2 ounces of melted white chocolate. Let the chocolate set for about 5 minutes in the refrigerator, then pour the curd over it.

ORANGE CREAMSICLE TART

GENERALLY SPEAKING, I AM NOT A BIG SODA DRINKER. In fact, the only time I ever really want a carbonated beverage is during a sour morning-after hangover. It wasn't always so. During the endless summers of grade school, I craved orange soda pop and only orange soda pop—no grape, no cola (certainly never water). This light, citrusy, summery tart is an elegant nod to my old obsession. It actually features orange soda as a main ingredient, yet the look and texture suggest something decidedly more upscale. It's soda-fountain quaint with a whiff of Le Cordon Bleu, and it is delicious.

YIELD: ONE 9-INCH TART

MAKE THE ORANGE CREAM SODA FILLING

Place the butter in a large bowl. Set aside.

In a wide bowl, sprinkle the gelatin evenly over the lemon juice (take care that the gelatin does not clump).

In a medium saucepan, stir together the orange juice and soda. Bring the liquid to a boil and cook until it is reduced by half, or 1 cup. Turn the heat to low and whisk to release excess heat.

In a medium bowl, whisk together the lemon and orange zest, eggs, egg yolks, and sugar and pour the mixture into the saucepan. Cook over medium-low heat, whisking constantly, until a candy thermometer reads 180 degrees F, or the curd can easily coats the back of a wooden spoon.

Remove the pan from the heat and add the gelatin mixture. Whisk until the gelatin is completely combined. Pour the liquid through a fine-mesh sieve directly onto the butter. Whisk the mixture furiously until it has increased a bit in volume (the faster you whisk, the more voluminous it will be). Cover the top of the curd with plastic wrap, pressing the plastic directly onto the curd's surface, and refrigerate for at least 4 hours.

MAKE THE ORANGE TART DOUGH

In the bowl of a standing mixer fitted with the paddle attachment, beat the butter, sugar, zest, and salt until light and fluffy. Add the egg, and beat just

until incorporated. Scrape down the bowl, add the flour all at once, and beat just until the dough comes together in a ball. Do not overbeat, or your crust will be hard.

Remove the dough from the bowl, shape it into a disk with your hands, wrap it tightly in plastic wrap, and refrigerate it for at least 30 minutes.

Dust a work surface with a sprinkling of flour. Use a rolling pin to roll the dough into a 10-inch circle about ¼ inch thick. (Note: The dough will be sticky. Make sure to turn it over with a bench knife or offset spatula as needed and to keep the work surface floured.)

Ever so gently, guide the dough, without pulling it, into a 9-inch tart pan with a removable bottom and lightly press it into place. Roll the rolling pin over the pan to trim off excess. Place the tart pan in the freezer for 30 minutes.

Preheat the oven to 375 degrees F.

Line the tart shell with aluminum foil and fill it three-quarters full with pie weights or dried beans. Bake for 15 minutes, then remove the foil and weights and bake for another 10 minutes, or until lightly browned. Transfer the tart pan to a wire rack to cool.

ASSEMBLE THE TART

In the bowl of a standing mixer fitted with the whisk attachment, beat the curd on high for 5 minutes, then spoon it into the tart and level the filling with an offset spatula. Refrigerate the tart for 1 hour to set completely.

MAKE THE ORANGE WHIPPED TOPPING

Pour the cream into a chilled metal bowl and beat it with a chilled whisk for about 1 minute. Sprinkle the sugar and orange cream soda on top and continue whisking vigorously until soft peaks form. (The whipped cream can be made in the bowl of a standing mixer fitted with the whisk attachment, but the hand-whisking method burns more calories. Also, if you prefer, you can substitute Simple Whipped Cream, page 159, for the flavored topping.)

To serve, gently push up on the tart bottom to release it from the pan. Top the tart with orange whipped cream.

The tart tastes best if eaten within 24 hours but can be kept, covered, in the refrigerator for up to 2 days.

BLACKBERRY PIE

AT THE AGE OF TWELVE, WHEN I CONSUMED ONE HEARTY PINT, ABOUT A WEEK'S WORTH, OF BLACKBERRIES IN TWENTY MINUTES, I WAS COMPLETELY UNAWARE THAT BERRIES, LIKE ALL FOOD, HAD A DISTINCT POINT OF ORIGIN. I just assumed that food came from a grocery store, that it was plentiful, and that it was universal. It was a revelation when I went to my first pick-your-own farm and I saw actual fruit on bushes and trees. It was also a revelation when I asked for the blackberry section of the farm and was told that I was a few states away from prime blackberry country. This pie is very straightforward and truly great with fresh, hand-picked blackberries (check out pickyourown.org for a comprehensive list of farms); however you will not taste the slightest hint of guilt if you get your blackberries via the grocery store route.

YIELD: ONE 9-INCH PIE

Ingredients

2 balls Classic Pie Dough (page 58)
1½ tablespoons fresh lemon juice
1½ teaspoons freshly grated lemon zest
¾ cup granulated sugar
⅓ cup firmly packed dark brown sugar
⅓ cup all-purpose flour
¼ teaspoon salt
7 cups fresh blackberries
1½ tablespoon butter, cut into 8 tiny pieces
1 large egg, beaten
1½ tablespoons raw cane sugar

Baked Note

Blackberries are sometimes labeled "Marionberries" or "Marion blackberries" as this is the most prolific commercial type of blackberry (especially in the western half of the United States). It is, essentially, a crossbred berry notable for both its taste and its production.

Dust a work surface with a sprinkling of flour. Roll out one of the balls of dough into a 12-inch round. Transfer the dough to a 9-inch pie plate and gently work it into place, folding any overhang under and crimping the edge as you go. Wrap and refrigerate the crust for at least 30 minutes.

Preheat the oven to 350 degrees F.

In a small bowl or cup, stir together the lemon juice and zest. In a large bowl, stir together the sugars, flour, and salt. Add the blackberries and gently toss everything together with your hands. Sprinkle the lemon juice mixture over the top of the berries and toss again. Pour the blackberry mixture into the prepared pie shell and scatter the pieces of butter over the top.

Dust a work surface with a sprinkling of flour. Roll the remaining ball of chilled dough into a 12-inch round and place it over the pie filling. Trim the dough, leaving about a ½-inch overhang. Crimp the edges together, brush with the beaten egg, and sprinkle with the raw sugar. Cut six long steam vents into the top crust. Bake the pie until the filling bubbles and the crust is golden, about 1 hour. Cool the pie on a rack for at least 1 hour. Serve warm or at room temperature.

The pie can be stored in the refrigerator, tightly covered, for up to 2 days. Bring it to room temperature or reheat it in a warm oven before serving.

Ingredients

FOR THE PEARS AND POACHING LIQUID

1 (15-ounce) can pear halves in heavy syrup, about 6 halves

1½ tablespoons fresh lemon juice

2 tablespoons whiskey

3 tablespoons sugar

1 tablespoon pure vanilla extract

FOR THE BASIC SWEET TART DOUGH

¼ cup sugar

1½ cups all-purpose flour

¼ teaspoon salt

½ cup (1 stick) cold unsalted butter, cut into ½-inch cubes

1 large egg, beaten

FOR THE ALMOND CREAM FILLING

¼ cup (½ stick) unsalted butter, cool but not cold

4½ ounces almond paste

1 large egg

1½ tablespoons cornstarch

1 tablespoon whiskey

FOR THE PEAR GLAZE

Reserved syrup and reserved "poaching" liquid from pears

1 teaspoon whiskey

¾ teaspoon cornstarch

WHISKEY PEAR TART

I BASICALLY BAKE WITH MY LIQUOR CABINET OPEN AND IN FULL VIEW. I PREFER FLAVORED LIQUEURS (KAHLÚA, FRAMBOISE, AND SO FORTH) OVER EXTRACTS (VANILLA EXTRACT EXCLUDED), AS THEY TEND TO BE MORE SUBTLE. Extracts tend to attack and take over a dessert. Liqueurs are content to stay in the background. Whiskey, on the other hand, is an entirely different dessert companion; it sexes things up with smoky undertones. I cannot imagine our pear tart sans whiskey. The pears take on a robustness and soul unlike their dainty teetotaler counterparts, and it cuts the sweetness of the almond cream filling just perfectly. Incidentally, I like to serve this tart for dessert alongside a shot of the same whiskey I used for baking.

This is a very easy recipe, but for the sake of making it easier, I broke it up into two parts. Since you have to "poach" the pears overnight, I suggest making the tart dough at the same time. The following day is a cinch: Just roll and bake the dough, and fill and bake the tart.

YIELD: ONE 14-BY-4-INCH RECTANGULAR TART

OR ONE 11-INCH ROUND TART

MAKE THE PEARS AND POACHING LIQUID

Strain the pears and reserve the heavy syrup (for the glaze) in a small, covered bowl or cup in the refrigerator.

In a medium, nonreactive bowl, whisk together the lemon juice, whiskey, sugar, and vanilla. Toss the pears with the liquid, cover the bowl tightly with plastic wrap, and refrigerate overnight.

MAKE THE SWEET TART DOUGH

Put the sugar, flour, and salt in a food processor and pulse until combined. Add the butter and pulse until sandy (about 6 to 10 quick pulses). Add the egg and pulse just until the dough begins to form a mass. Form the dough into a disk, wrap it tightly in plastic, and refrigerate it overnight (or for at least 1 hour).

BAKE THE CRUST

Dust a work surface with a sprinkling of flour. Use a rolling pin to roll the

dough about ¼ inch thick into either a rectangle about 15 inches long or into a round about 12 inches in diameter. (Note: The dough will be sticky. Make sure to turn it with a bench knife or offset spatula as needed and keep the working surface floured. Some people find it easier to roll dough between two layers of plastic wrap. This can ease transfer and be a bit less messy.)

Ever so gently, guide the dough into the tart pan, without pulling it, and lightly press it into place. Roll the rolling pin over the pan to trim off excess dough. Place the tart pan in the freezer for 30 minutes.

Preheat the oven to 375 degrees F.

Line the tart shell with aluminum foil and fill it three-quarters full with pie weights or dried beans. Bake for 15 minutes, then remove the foil and weights and bake for another 10 minutes, or until lightly browned. Transfer the tart pan to a wire rack to cool. Leave the oven on.

MAKE THE ALMOND CREAM FILLING

In the bowl of a standing mixer fitted with the paddle attachment, cream the butter and almond paste on medium speed until the mixture is light, fluffy, and smooth, 3 to 4 minutes. Add the egg and beat until combined. Sprinkle the cornstarch over the filling and turn the mixer to low. Drizzle in the whiskey and beat until it is combined. Spread the almond cream filling evenly over the cooled tart shell.

Drain the pear halves, reserving the soaking liquid, and arrange them decoratively on top of the almond cream. Bake for 35 to 40 minutes, or until the almond cream puffs up and sets and the crust turns golden brown. Let the tart cool on a wire rack while you make the glaze.

MAKE THE PEAR GLAZE

Place the syrup and soaking liquid in a medium pan over medium heat and gently boil until the liquid is reduced to about ¾ cup. Remove it from the heat and whisk quickly and continuously for 1 minute to speed cooling. Add the whiskey and cornstarch and whisk to combine. Set the pan over medium-high heat, bring the glaze to a boil, and cook it for 1 minute. Use a pastry brush to apply the glaze gently to the tart.

Remove the tart from the pan and serve it as soon as possible. The tart will keep at room temperature, covered, for up to 3 days, but the crust will turn slightly soggy after the first day.

HOW TO POACH YOUR OWN PEARS

Suffice it to say, there are many, many ways to poach your own pears. You can use a variety of liquids (water, wine, half water/half wine, diluted fruit juice), and you can tweak the liquid according to your mood (add spices, other fruits, vanilla, and sugars). It is a recipe with endless possibilities, and I suggest you modify the below ingredients at will. This quick poaching method is only a roadmap, so feel free to throw your personality in the poaching pot:

4 firm and ripe pears
1 cup sugar
1 bottle of cheap and cheerful sweet dry wine
Zest and juice of 1 orange

Peel the pears, core them, and cut them in half. Set aside.

In a large saucepan set over low heat, stir together the sugar and the wine until dissolved.

Stir in the orange zest and juice, increase the heat to medium, and wait for the liquid to simmer.

Once the liquid reaches a low boil, add the pears and simmer for 15–30 minutes. During the poaching process it is important to make sure the liquid covers the pears the entire time.

The pears are done when a sharp knife inserted into the bulbous end of the pear slides in and out easily. Check your pears every few minutes after the 15-minute mark, as cooking time is determined by the size and ripeness of your pears.

Remove the pears and let cool if you are using in a recipe, or serve warm with any accompaniment (ice cream, whipped cream, etc.). The poaching liquid can be reused. Store the poaching liquid in an airtight container in the refrigerator for up to 1 week.

Ingredients

FOR THE TASSIE SHELLS

1 cup (2 sticks) unsalted butter, softened,
cut into ½-inch cubes

6 ounces cream cheese, softened,
cut into 1-inch cubes

1 tablespoon sugar

2 cups all-purpose flour

FOR THE TASSIE FILLING

2 large eggs

1½ cups firmly packed light brown sugar

2 tablespoons pure vanilla extract

⅛ teaspoon salt

1 cup toasted pecans, coarsely chopped

Baked Note

It is worth noting that many heritage-type recipes were transcribed in the days before the standing mixer. This seems obvious, but it never really occurred to me until I started to sort through people's archives. This pecan tassie recipe is adapted directly from my aunt, but I updated it to make use of a standing mixer (and a few other modern items). If you want to do it the authentic way, simply blend the crust ingredients with a fork.

PECAN TASSIES

TRACKING DOWN THE ORIGIN OF A RECIPE IS A TASK BEST SUITED TO THE MOST DOGGED REPORTER. A recipe might begin in one state, be adopted by another, and then manipulated by a third. Following the winding trail might be an insurmountable task, and that is why I will not argue with my Aunt Judy, from upstate New York, about her pecan tassies. She insists, in a very proud way, that it is a local regional recipe. I happen to believe it is from the South. We will never know who is right, because pecan tassie information is scarce. There are virtually no stories or lore (at least none that I can find) surrounding these mini desserts, yet I always assumed the tassie emerged from some heritage holiday collection. A pecan tassie is essentially a miniature, gooey, pecan pie with a hassle-free crust. They are transportable, individual, and picturesque. I doubt they will ever completely satisfy a pecan pie craving (the crust-to-filling ratio of the full-size pie is nearly perfect), but they will certainly tide you over.

YIELD: ABOUT **40** TASSIES

MAKE THE TASSIE SHELLS

In the bowl of a standing mixer fitted with the paddle attachment, beat the butter and cream cheese together on medium speed until the mixture is lump free. Add the sugar and beat again for 15 seconds. Scrape down the bottom and sides of the bowl. Add the flour in four parts, at low speed, until the mixture is just combined and a dough forms. Pinch off a walnut-size piece of dough, roll it into a ball, and set it aside. Continue pinching and rolling until all the dough is gone. You will end up with approximately 40 pieces. Place each ball into an individual mini muffin pan, then use your fingers to press the dough into the bottom and up the sides of each pan.

Once all the tassie shells have been formed, place the muffin pan in the refrigerator while you make the filling.

Preheat the oven to 350 degrees F.

MAKE THE TASSIE FILLING

In a medium bowl, whisk the eggs just until they break apart. While whisking, gradually add the brown sugar until completely combined. Add the vanilla and salt and whisk again. Add ½ cup of the chopped pecans and stir until they are completely mixed in.

ASSEMBLE THE TASSIES

Sprinkle the remaining ½ cup pecans into the tassie shells. Spoon in enough filling into the shells until they are about three-quarters full.

Bake for about 15 minutes. Reduce the oven temperature to 250 degrees F, and bake for another 10 minutes, or until the filling is set.

Allow the tassies to cool for at least 30 minutes. Serve them warm or at room temperature. Pecan tassies taste best the day they are made; however, you can wrap them in plastic and keep them at room temperature for up to 2 days.

HOW TO TOAST NUTS

There are two ways to toast nuts: the oven method and the skillet method. Both are easy.

Oven Method Preheat your oven to 300 degrees F. Spread the nuts in an even layer on a rimmed baking sheet and toast until fragrant. (Be sure to toss and flip your nuts half-way through the baking process).

Estimated Baking Times for Different Nuts	
5 minutes	*pine nuts aka pignolis*
10 minutes	*almonds (sliced and whole), pecans, and walnuts*
12 minutes	*hazelnuts and macadamia*

Skillet Method (I actually prefer this method.) Place the nuts in a single layer in a large skillet set over medium heat. Stir and flip the nuts frequently until fragrant and almost golden. Usually, the nuts will toast more quickly (about half the time listed above) using this method; however, keep a keen nose at the ready, as toasting times will vary depending on heat source.

3

 COOKIES AND BARS

I rarely make use of my two cookie jars. One is a basic, perfectly adequate, glass jar with the latest in airtight technology. The other is heavy ceramic, shaped and painted to resemble an art deco gas pump (file under the strange things we accumulate). Both are gathering dust. For a few reasons, I never make more cookies than are immediately required. First, cookies really do taste best the day they are made or, even better, straight from the oven. I recommend that bakers refrigerate almost any dough and bake it as needed. Second, I am lazy. Most recipes yield several dozen cookies, yet I only like to bake one or two dozen at a time. I do not have the patience to endure more than one bake cycle. Lastly, I love cookies too much. I possess little self-control if a chocolate chip, a black and white, or the much-beloved cowboy cookie is lurking nearby. If I bake twelve cookies, chances are I will eat twelve cookies, unless there is someone around to share them with.

Thankfully, my willpower isn't tested by bar cookies or brownies. For some reason, my brain views a bar cookie (at least when left in its original baking receptacle) as part of a larger whole, something that would have to be consumed en masse if eaten at all. Better to just slice a bit off, remove it from the baking dish, move far away, and forget about the rest.

I really enjoy making bars in the same way that I like making casserole-type dishes for potluck dinner parties.

They are easy to tote about, a little bit homey, usually not too time-consuming, and delicious (if you use the right recipe). Regretfully, bar cookies (and, to some degree, cookies of any type), make only brief appearances in the realm of storied five-star desserts. Odd how ice cream is currently celebrated and critically acclaimed on several fine-dining menus, yet brownies are still considered the handiwork of a "fern bar" or "quick casual" restaurant. Life is unfair.

The cookie and bar recipes throughout this chapter are informed by some of the most interesting stories and lore in the entire book. The Joe Frogger (see page 127), a wonderful ginger molasses cookie, has a backstory that borders on Hollywoodesque, and the Cowboy Cookie (see page 91), while completely addictive, probably has nothing to do with cowboys. I enjoyed all the research that went into this chapter, and I had an even better time testing (i.e., eating) my way through the recipes. I hope you have as much fun as I did...and don't miss the Grasshopper Bars (see page 97).

Ingredients

FOR THE CHOCOLATE MINT
THUMBPRINTS

*2 ounces good-quality dark chocolate
(60 to 72%)*

*2 ounces mint chocolate (or Andes mint
chocolate candies)*

1½ cups all-purpose flour

*½ cup dark unsweetened cocoa powder
(like Valrhona)*

¾ teaspoon salt

*1 cup (2 sticks) unsalted butter, cut into
1-inch cubes, at room temperature*

⅓ cup granulated sugar

*2 tablespoons firmly packed dark
brown sugar*

2 large egg yolks

1 teaspoon pure vanilla extract

1 cup coarse sugar for rolling

FOR THE WHITE CHOCOLATE
FILLING

*3 ounces good-quality white chocolate,
coarsely chopped*

3 tablespoons heavy cream

½ teaspoon pure peppermint extract

Baked Note

If you want a perfect thumbprint in every
cookie (and in order to avoid burning
yourself), feel free to use the handle
of a wooden spoon to make the initial
indentation and subsequent one. It also
makes the whole process slightly faster.

CHOCOLATE MINT THUMBPRINTS

THE PROBLEM WITH CATEGORIZING CERTAIN COOKIES AS "HOLIDAY" OR "CHRISTMAS" TREATS IS THAT IT TENDS TO PREVENT A GREAT RECIPE FROM BEING USED YEARROUND. That is a tragedy, especially if the cookie is as addictive as our Chocolate Mint Thumbprint. I originally made these cookies for a magazine's holiday story (hence the presence of mint), but I now find myself whipping them up for almost any occasion. The chocolate cookie base is perfectly textured—crunchy, crumbly—not too sweet, and the filling is a simple, creamy, white chocolate peppermint ganache (make sure you use a high-quality white chocolate).

YIELD: ABOUT **40** COOKIES

MAKE THE CHOCOLATE MINT THUMBPRINTS

Melt the dark chocolate and mint chocolate together in a microwave or over a double boiler (see page 16). Whisk until smooth, then set aside to cool.

In a medium bowl, whisk together the flour, cocoa powder, and salt. Set aside.

In the bowl of a standing mixer fitted with the paddle attachment, beat the butter until creamy. Add the granulated and brown sugars and beat on medium-high speed until light and fluffy, about 3 minutes. Add the egg yolks and vanilla and beat again until combined. Scrape the chocolate into the mixer and beat just until incorporated. Scrape down the sides and bottom of the bowl and add the flour mixture all at once. Beat on low speed, scraping the side of the bowl occasionally, until the dough is smooth. Transfer it to a sheet of plastic wrap and pat it into a disk; wrap and refrigerate it until it is chilled and firm, at least 30 minutes.

Preheat the oven to 350 degrees F. Line two baking sheets with parchment paper.

Pour the coarse sugar into a shallow bowl.

With clean hands, form tablespoon-size dough balls, taking care that they have no lumps or cracks. Roll each ball in the coarse sugar and place it on a

prepared baking sheet. Use your thumb or a small dowel to make an indentation in the center of the cookie. Bake for 10 minutes, remove the sheet from the oven, and use your thumb or the dowel to make the indentation more visible. Return the sheets to the oven and bake for another 4 to 5 minutes. (These are the type of cookies that can overbake very quickly—pull them out at the first signs of cracking.) Set the baking sheets on a wire rack to cool for 5 minutes. Use a spatula to transfer the cookies to the rack to cool completely before filling them.

MAKE THE WHITE CHOCOLATE FILLING

Place the white chocolate in a glass measuring cup with a pour spout. Put the cream in a microwave-safe bowl or cup and microwave it on high power until it boils, about 30 seconds. Pour the hot cream over the white chocolate and let stand for 30 seconds, then whisk until smooth. Stir in the peppermint extract. Fill the thumbprint cookies with the white chocolate ganache and refrigerate them until set, about 30 minutes.

These cookies taste great at room temperature or directly from the refrigerator. They can be stored in an airtight container in the refrigerator for up to 3 days.

COWBOY COOKIES

THE NAME, COWBOY COOKIE, IS A BIT FANTASTICAL. I mean, I am fairly certain that there is only just the faintest hint of connection (if any) between actual cowboys and these cookies. My basic, modest research cannot find a reference anywhere stating that they were invented by cowboys, enjoyed by cowboys, or made in honor of cowboys. It seems the name is simply a sly reference to the rugged manliness implied by the cookie's bigness and embrace-it-all ingredients.

Whatever their origins, they are delicious. The typical components of the cowboy cookie are oatmeal, chocolate chips, walnuts or pecans, crunchy exterior, and chewy interior. Ours is slightly different. I opted to do away with the nuts and added salty pretzels; we also tossed in some instant espresso powder to add a grown-up (maybe cowboyish) flavor.

YIELD: MAKES ABOUT 36 COOKIES

Ingredients

1¾ cups all-purpose flour

1 teaspoon baking soda

1 teaspoon baking powder

½ teaspoon salt

2 cups rolled oats

14 tablespoons (1¾ sticks) unsalted butter, cool but not cold, cut into 1-inch cubes

¾ cup granulated sugar

1 cup firmly packed dark brown sugar

1 large egg

1 large egg yolk

1 teaspoon vanilla extract

1 teaspoon instant espresso powder

2 cups semisweet chocolate chunks (about 12 ounces)

¾ cup thin salty pretzels (about 1½ ounces), broken into tiny pieces but not crushed into dust

In a medium bowl, whisk together the flour, baking soda, baking powder, and salt. Add the oats and stir to combine.

In the bowl of a standing mixer fitted with the paddle attachment, beat the butter and sugars together until smooth and creamy. Add the egg and egg yolk, beating until the mixture looks light and fluffy. Scrape down the sides and bottom of the bowl, add the vanilla, and beat for 5 seconds. Dissolve the espresso powder in ¼ cup hot water and add it to the bowl, mixing until combined.

Add half of the dry ingredients and mix for 15 seconds. Add the remaining dry ingredients and beat until just incorporated. Scrape down the sides and bottom of the bowl and fold in the chocolate chunks and ½ cup of the pretzel pieces.

Cover the bowl tightly and refrigerate the dough for at least 4 hours.

Preheat the oven to 350 degrees F. Line two baking sheets with parchment paper.

Use a small ice cream scoop with a release mechanism to scoop out dough in 2 tablespoon–size balls (or use a tablespoon measure) and place the dough balls

Baked Note

This recipe (and a few others in this book) calls for cool, but not cold butter. To be specific, I am suggesting you remove the butter from the refrigerator, cut it up into cubes, and plan to use it within 15 to 20 minutes. Using colder (i.e. not room temperature) butter will prevent your cookies from spreading. Conversely, if you prefer thinner, slightly crispier cookies, let your butter come to room temperature.

onto the prepared baking sheet about 1 inch apart. Sprinkle the remaining ¼ cup pretzel pieces over the dough balls. Use the palm of your hand to press the dough down lightly; don't smash the cookie—you just want to slightly flatten the ball and push the pretzel pieces into the dough.

Bake for 11 to 13 minutes, rotating the pans halfway through the baking time, until the edges of the cookies are golden brown or just start to darken.

Set the pan on a wire rack for 10 minutes to cool. Use a spatula to transfer the cookies to the rack to cool completely. They can be stored in an airtight container for up to 3 days (though I doubt they will last that long).

SWEET & SALTY BROWNIE

THE GENESIS BEHIND THE FORMATION OF OUR BAKERY, BAKED, WAS TO ELEVATE THE CLASSIC AMERICAN BROWNIE FROM UBIQUITOUS MEDIOCRITY TO BONA FIDE LUXURY. It is brownie as fetish. The Sweet & Salty Brownie is the Baked brownie in extreme, a decadence on par with other, more well-known (and perhaps more respected) desserts. The brownie itself is a riff on our famous deep, dark brownie (sans instant espresso powder) filled with a smoky, dark caramel and topped with just a hint of sea salt and sugar. The caramel taste is more of a hint and less of an explosion, befitting this elegant dessert; the result is a fudgey-chocolatey-carameley brownie. I should also reveal that the Sweet & Salty Brownie is our most requested recipe, owing to the brownie's featured moment on the Food Network, where it was lauded with praise as one of the best salty foods in the United States. That is a lot of hype for one brownie, but in this case, I think it is worthy.

YIELD: 12 LARGE BROWNIES OR 24 SMALL BROWNIES

MAKE THE CARAMEL

In a medium saucepan, combine the sugar and corn syrup with ¼ cup water, stirring them together carefully so you don't splash the sides of the pan. Cook over high heat until an instant-read thermometer reads 350 degrees F, or until the mixture is dark amber in color (keep a close eye on the caramel at all times, as it goes from golden brown to black and burnt very quickly), 6 to 8 minutes. Remove for the heat, and slowly add the cream (careful, it will bubble up) and then the fleur de sel. Whisk in the sour cream. Set aside to cool.

MAKE THE BROWNIE

Preheat oven to 350 degrees F.

Butter the sides and bottom of a glass or light-colored metal 9-by-13-inch pan. Line the bottom with a sheet of parchment paper, and butter the parchment.

In a medium bowl, whisk together the flour, salt, and cocoa powder.

Place the chocolate and butter in the bowl of the double boiler set over a pan of simmering water, and stir occasionally until the chocolate and butter are completely melted and combined. Turn off the heat, but keep the bowl over

Ingredients

FOR THE FILLING

1 cup sugar

2 tablespoons light corn syrup

½ cup heavy cream

1 teaspoon fleur de sel

¼ cup sour cream

FOR THE BROWNIE

1¼ cups all-purpose flour

1 teaspoon salt

2 tablespoons dark unsweetened cocoa powder (like Valrhona)

11 ounces quality dark chocolate (60 to 72%), coarsely chopped

1 cup (2 sticks) unsalted butter, cut into 1-inch cubes

1½ cups sugar

½ cup firmly packed light brown sugar

5 large eggs, at room temperature

2 teaspoons vanilla extract

FOR THE ASSEMBLY

1½ teaspoons fleur de sel

1 teaspoon coarse sugar

Baked Note

That old adage "less is more" holds true here. You might be tempted to add more caramel than recommended, but temper your indulgence. If you build too much of a caramel layer, it more than likely will seep out and burn during baking. In fact this recipe will make more than enough caramel for one batch of brownies. If you are a caramel addict, use the extra to drizzle on the brownie post-baking/pre-serving.

the water of the double boiler, and add both sugars. Whisk until completely combined and remove the bowl from the pan. The mixture should be at room temperature.

Add three eggs to the chocolate mixture and whisk until just combined. Add the remaining eggs and whisk until just combined. Add the vanilla and stir until combined. Do not overbeat the batter at this stage, or your brownies will be cakey.

Sprinkle the flour mixture over the chocolate. Using a spatula, fold the dry ingredients into the wet ingredients until there is just a trace amount of the flour mixture visible.

ASSEMBLE THE SWEET & SALTY BROWNIE

Pour half of the brownie mixture into the pan and smooth the top with a spatula. Drizzle about ¾ cup of the caramel sauce over the brownie layer in a zigzag pattern, taking care to make sure the caramel does not come in contact with the edges of the pan or it will burn. Use your offset spatula to spread the caramel evenly across the brownie layer. In heaping spoonfuls, scoop the rest of the brownie batter over the caramel layer. Smooth the brownie batter gently to cover the caramel layer.

Bake the brownies for 30 minutes, rotating the pan halfway through the baking time, and check to make sure the brownies are completely done by sticking a toothpick into the center of the pan. The brownies are done when the toothpick comes out with a few moist crumbs.

Remove the brownies from the oven and sprinkle with the fleur de sel and coarse sugar.

Cool the brownies completely before cutting and serving.

The brownies can be stored, tightly wrapped at room temperature, for up to 4 days.

FREEZING BROWNIES

Brownies, unlike many bar cookies, freeze particularly well. In fact, some brownie fanatics claim freezing improves the texture. I am still undecided. Regardless, there is an art to freezing your brownies to avoid the sticky, sweaty surface condensation.

1. Allow the brownies to cool to room temperature. Wrap your room temperature brownies in two layers of plastic wrap. It is best to wrap the brownies directly as opposed to wrapping the pan of brownies. Place your brownies in the freezer.

2. When you are ready to defrost your brownies, remove them from the freezer and place them in the refrigerator for 8 hours or overnight. Then remove the brownies from the refrigerator and let them sit at room temperature for at least 1 hour.

3. Unwrap and eat your brownies.

Generally speaking, brownies will keep in the freezer for up to 1 month, but I know people who have kept them far beyond that threshold and have lived to tell about it.

GRASSHOPPER BARS

THE BAKED GRASSHOPPER BAR WAS SUPPOSED TO BE A SHORT-LIVED EXPERIMENT, A QUIRKY RIFF ON THE MINTY CLASSIC 1950S COCKTAIL WITH WHICH WE ARE SLIGHTLY OBSESSED. The impulse to make it came from a cookbook my mom had stashed away, an ancient tome with an emphasis on Midwestern cuisine. Unfortunately, the only thing it seemed to have going for it was page after page of hideous gelatin-infused recipes, each more gruesome than the one before. Still, something about the grasshopper pie was intriguing. Even though the original tastes like medicinal Jell-O, we persevered through countless iterations. And the bar, which was supposed to be just a jokey tongue-in-cheek confection, has endured. The layers work in perfect harmony: thick brownie base, light mint filling, and a dark ganache top. Interestingly enough, this sweet treat works equally well as a classy plated dessert and as an after-school snack.

→ YIELD: 12 LARGE BROWNIES OR 24 SMALL BROWNIES ←

MAKE THE BROWNIE BASE

Preheat the oven to 325 degrees F.

Butter the sides and bottom of a glass or light-colored metal 9-by-13-inch pan. Line the bottom with a sheet of parchment paper, and butter the parchment. In a medium bowl, whisk together the flour, the salt, and cocoa powder.

Configure a large size double boiler. Place the chocolate and the butter in the bowl of the double boiler and stir occasionally until the chocolate and butter are completely melted and combined. Turn off the heat, but keep the bowl over the water of the double boiler and add both sugars. Whisk the sugars until completely combined. Remove the bowl from the pan. The mixture should be at room temperature.

Add three eggs to the chocolate/butter mixture and whisk until just combined. Add the vanilla and stir until combined. Do not overbeat the batter at this stage or your brownies will be cakey.

Sprinkle the flour/cocoa/salt mix over the chocolate. Using a spatula (do not use a whisk) fold the dry ingredients into the wet until there is just a trace amount of the flour/cocoa mix visible.

Ingredients

FOR THE BROWNIE BASE

¾ cups flour

½ teaspoon salt

1 tablespoon dark unsweetened cocoa powder (like Valrhona)

5 ounces good quality dark chocolate (60 to 72%), coarsely chopped

½ cup (1 stick) butter, cut into 1 inch cubes

¾ cup sugar

¼ cup firmly packed light brown sugar

3 large eggs, at room temperature

1 teaspoons vanilla extract

FOR THE BUTTERCREAM

¾ cup sugar

2 tablespoons flour

¾ cup milk

2 tablespoons heavy cream

1½ sticks (¾ cup) butter, softened but still cool, cut into small cubes

3 tablespoons crème de menthe

1 teaspoon peppermint extract

FOR THE CHOCOLATE GLAZE

6 ounces good-quality dark chocolate (60 to 72%) coarsely chopped

1 teaspoon light corn syrup

½ cup (1 stick) unsalted butter, softened, cut into cubes

Baked Note

I rarely advocate underbaking in the quest to develop texture (the raw cookie dough thing was never my cup of tea); however, many of my recipe testers admitted to underbaking the brownie base portion of this recipe by just a few minutes. I tried it, and I admit a fudgier texture is a nice option. The recipe is written for the full baking time, but the final decision is yours.

Pour the batter into the prepared pan, smooth the top with an offset spatula, and bake for approximately 12 to 15 minutes, rotating halfway through the baking time. The brownies should be just a tad underdone (not too gooey, but ideally, just 1 minute from being cooked through completely). A toothpick inserted into the brownies at an angle should contain a few loose crumbs. Remove the brownies from the oven and let cool completely while you make the creme de menthe filling.

MAKE THE BUTTERCREAM

In a medium heavy-bottomed saucepan, whisk the sugar and flour together. Add the milk and cream and cook over medium heat, whisking occasionally until mixture comes to a boil and has thickened, 5 to 7 minutes.

Transfer the mixture to the bowl of an electric mixer fitted with the paddle attachment. Beat on high speed until cool. Reduce the speed to low and add the butter and mix until thoroughly incorporated. Increase the speed to medium-high and beat until filling is light and fluffy.

Add the crème de menthe and peppermint extract and mix until combined. If the filling is too soft, chill slightly in the refrigerator and then mix again until it is the proper consistency.

If the filling is too firm, place the bowl over a pot of simmering water and re-mix to proper consistency. Spread the filling evenly across the top of the brownie layer and place the pan in the refrigerator, for a minimum of 45 minutes, while you make the chocolate glaze.

MAKE THE CHOCOLATE GLAZE

In a large non-reactive metal bowl, combine the chocolate, corn syrup, and butter. Set the bowl over a saucepan of simmering water and cook, stirring with a rubber spatula, until the mixture is completely smooth. Remove the bowl from the pan and stir vigorously for 1 minute to release excess heat.

Pour the mixture over the chilled crème de menthe layer and use an offset spatula to spread it into an even layer. Place the pan back in the refrigerator for 1 hour, or until the glaze hardens.

Remove the pan from the refrigerator, wait about 15 minutes for the glaze to soften slightly, and cut the bars with a warm knife. Cut into squares and serve immediately.

The bars can be stored in the refrigerated, tightly covered, for up to 4 days.

HEARTLAND TURTLE BARS

THIS TURTLE BAR RECIPE WAS PASSED ON TO ME BY A NEWFOUND ACQUAINTANCE I ENCOUNTERED WHILE TRAVELING ALONG THE BORDER OF SOUTH DAKOTA AND IOWA. She assured me that the bar came from the heartland—she dug up the recipe some time ago from one of those church cookbooks, which she found in Minnesota. These bars are wonderfully addictive snacks. I suppose the oatmeal in the crust is my favorite part, and it's what sets this bar apart from other "turtle" offerings.

YIELD: 24 BARS

MAKE THE BAR TOPPING AND BASE

Preheat the oven to 350 degrees F. Butter the sides and bottom of a 9-by-13-inch glass or light-colored metal baking pan. Line the pan with parchment paper so that the paper overhangs the pan on two sides. Butter the parchment. In a medium bowl, whisk together the flour, salt, and baking soda. Use your hands to rub in the brown sugar. Add the oats and stir until the ingredients are evenly combined. Make a well in the center of the dry ingredients, then pour in the melted butter and stir until the entire mixture is wet and combined.

Spread two-thirds of the mixture across the bottom of the prepared pan and bake for about 10 minutes. Remove the pan from the oven to cool (but leave the oven on). Sprinkle the pecans and chocolate chips across the cooled crust.

MAKE THE CARAMEL FILLING

In a medium saucepan over medium-high heat, melt the sugar and butter together. Bring the mixture to a boil and boil for 1 minute, stirring constantly (the caramel will begin to darken quickly at this point). Remove the pan from the heat, stir in the cream, and pour the caramel directly over the chocolate pecan layer. Use an offset spatula to evenly distribute the caramel. Sprinkle the remaining oatmeal mixture onto the caramel and bake for 10 to 12 minutes, or until the top is golden brown.

Let the bars cool in the pan for about 15 minutes, then place the pan in the refrigerator and chill for 1 hour to firm up. Cut and serve. The bars can be stored, tightly wrapped, in the refrigerator or at room temperature for up to 3 days.

Ingredients

FOR THE BAR TOPPING AND BASE

1½ cups all-purpose flour

¼ teaspoon salt

¾ teaspoon baking soda

1 cup firmly packed dark brown sugar

1¾ cups rolled oats

1 cup (2 sticks) unsalted butter, melted

1 cup toasted pecans, chopped into large pieces

1½ cups chocolate chips

FOR THE CARAMEL FILLING

½ cup firmly packed light brown sugar

10 tablespoons (1¼ sticks) unsalted butter, cut into cubes

2 tablespoons heavy cream

Baked Note

This is quite a buttery dessert. I, personally, have never found anything too buttery (I would be happy to use an entire stick on one bagel), but if you want to cut back on the butter in this recipe, leave out a tablespoon or two in the oatmeal crust. Just remember, this is a heritage recipe—avoid substituting margarine at all costs.

Baked Note

In this recipe, I suggest using a 2-inch
round cookie cutter; however, it is only for
guidance. Obviously, you can use any size,
shape, and type of cookie cutter you fancy
or have on hand. Also, note that while I
prefer a crisp ¼-inch cookie, I have plenty
of friends that like them a bit thicker and
chewier. If you are like them, simply roll
out the dough to ½ inch thick and bake the
cookies for a minute less.

SALT-N-PEPPER SANDWICH COOKIES

I SUPPOSE THE BAKED OBSESSION WITH COOKIE SANDWICHES IS BUILT ON THE MEMORY AND ENDURANCE OF THE OREO. The Oreo, a cookie only the American palate could love, was probably created in our hometown of New York City (at the Nabisco factory in Chelsea), though it is hardly a regional treat anymore. There is no sense in trying to upgrade, tweak, or improve upon this American icon, and it should be left undisturbed. So, consider this recipe a mere tribute. The chocolate sandwich cookies are crisp and toothsome, with a hint of salt and pepper that works beautifully with the cocoa powder, and we filled the whole thing with a pretty close approximation of the classic Oreo filling, sans trans fats and other chemical no-nos. Unlike the original, these do not cry out to be dunked in milk, and they actually make a rather chic after-dinner treat.

YIELD: APPROXIMATELY 36 COOKIE SANDWICHES

MAKE THE COOKIES

In a large bowl, sift together the flour, salt, fleur de sel, white pepper, and cocoa powder. Set aside.

In the bowl of a standing mixer fitted with the paddle attachment, beat the butter and sugars together until light and fluffy, about 3 minutes. Scrape down the bowl, and add the egg yolks, one at a time, beating until each is incorporated. Add the vanilla and melted chocolate and beat until uniform in color. Scrape down the sides and bottom of the bowl and beat again for 10 seconds.

Add half of the dry ingredients and beat for 15 seconds. Again, scrape down the bowl, add the remaining dry ingredients and beat until just incorporated.

Loosely shape the dough into two balls, wrap them tightly in plastic wrap, and refrigerate them for at least 3 hours.

Preheat the oven to 350 degrees F. Line two baking sheets with parchment paper.

SALT-N-PEPPER AND MALTED MILK SANDWICH COOKIES (PAGE 106)

Unwrap one ball of dough and divide it into two equal portions. Place the first portion on a lightly flour-dusted work surface and return the other to the refrigerator.

Use your hands to knead the dough until pliable and form into a small disc. Roll the dough into a ¼-inch-thick round. It will be slightly sticky, so you may have to flip and lightly flour it a few times while you work. Use a 2-inch round cookie cutter to create your sandwich tops and bottoms, and transfer them to the prepared baking sheets, leaving about 1 inch of space around each cookie. Continue the process with the remaining dough. Extra dough scraps can be refrigerated and rerolled, if desired.

Sprinkle the tops of the cookies with a little fleur de sel, then bake them for 10 to 12 minutes, rotating the sheets halfway through the baking time. The tops of the cookies should look a bit dry and possibly cracked. Place the baking sheets on wire racks to cool for 5 minutes. Use a spatula to transfer the cookies to the racks to cool completely before filling them.

MAKE THE VANILLA FILLING

In the bowl of a standing mixer fitted with the paddle attachment, beat the shortening and butter until lump free and smooth. Add the sugar in three parts, mixing each part until just combined. Add the salt, vanilla, and rum and beat again for 10 seconds. The filling should be thick but spreadable (like the inside of an Oreo). If it is too thick, add a drop or two of water as needed. Keep adding water to reach the desired consistency, but do not add too much water or the filling will be too thin.

Alternatively if the mixture is too thin, add a few tablespoons of confectioners' sugar.

ASSEMBLE THE SALT-N-PEPPER SANDWICH COOKIES

Use a pastry bag or a small spoon to apply about 2 tablespoons of filling to the flat side of a cookie. Place another cookie, flat side down, on top. Press down slightly so that the filling spreads to the edges of the cookie. Repeat until all the sandwich cookies are made. Let them set up for about 15 minutes before serving. Store the cookies at room temperature in an airtight container for up to 3 days.

CLASSIC SHORTBREAD
WITH FLEUR DE SEL

I HAVE SCOTTISH ROOTS. My paternal grandmother was originally from a small town just outside of Edinburgh, and she was steadfast in defending Scottish cuisine to her American children and grandchildren. It was not an easy battle. Her haggis, the classic Scottish dish made of many interior sheep parts, while probably the best haggis ever made, rarely won support or adulation at our family dinner table. But Grandma was persistent. She cooked through a veritable catalog of Scottish dishes before finally winning us over with mountains of classic, buttery, crispy shortbread. It was her mother's recipe, and she baked it with devotion. I grew to accept shortbread as part of the American cookie spectrum. The original recipe calls for an egg yolk to be spread over the rolled out dough and folded in gently by overlapping the dough into the egg. The idea is very interesting, but I still opted for the standing mixer route. Otherwise, the recipe is as written almost eighty years ago (the fleur de sel is my addition).

YIELD: ABOUT **48** COOKIES

In the bowl of a standing mixer fitted with the paddle attachment, beat the butter on high speed until smooth. Add the sugar and salt and beat again just until incorporated, about 2 minutes. In two additions, using a wooden spoon or the absolute lowest speed on your mixer, stir in 3½ cups of the all-purpose flour and all the rice flour, just until incorporated. Add the egg yolks, one at a time, and stir just until combined. If the dough looks too wet, fold in the remaining 2 tablespoons flour. Turn the dough out onto a lightly floured surface, and knead until it is uniform. Do not overwork it. Divide the dough into eight equal balls, then shape them into disks, wrap them in plastic, and refrigerate until firm, at least 1 hour.

Preheat the oven to 325 degrees F. Line two baking sheets with parchment paper.

Dust a work surface with a sprinkling of flour. Working with one piece of chilled dough at a time while leaving the others in the refrigerator, roll a disk into a slightly less than ½-inch round. Cut the round into wedges like a pizza.

Ingredients

1 pound (4 sticks) unsalted butter, cut into ½-inch cubes, cool but not cold

1 cup plus 2 tablespoons superfine sugar, or 1 cup confectioners' sugar

½ teaspoon salt

3½ cups plus 2 tablespoons all-purpose flour

½ cup rice flour

2 egg yolks

1 tablespoon fleur de sel

Baked Note

Shortbread is fickle, or at least complicated. I baked this recipe about thirty times, and each time the cookies tasted different than before. Finally, I hit shortbread nirvana. My advice: pay careful attention to the starting temperature of the butter. It should be cool, but not directly out of the refrigerator. And when I say "cut the butter into cubes," I mean you should really cut it into cubes. No irregular chunks, rectangles, or other shortcuts.

Prick the top of the shortbread with the tines of a fork and sprinkle a bit of fleur de sel over the surface. Transfer the cookies to a prepared baking sheet. Bake the shortbread for 17 to 22 minutes, or until they just begin to brown.

Set the pans on a wire rack to cool for 10 minutes before transferring the shortbreads to the rack to cool completely.

Shortbread will keep in an airtight container, at room temperature, for 5 days.

ALTERATIONS AND OTHER SHORTBREAD SINS

I am fairly certain that my grandmother's eyes would pop out of her head at the mere suggestion of adding anything to her classic shortbread recipe. She might sniff at the idea of a chocolate dip as "unnecessarily rich" and introducing flavors into the mix as "missing the point." It is with this knowledge, that I offer a few riffs on the classic shortbread. Apologies to grandma in advance.

Chocolate Dip Line a baking sheet with parchment paper. Melt about 8 to 10 ounces of good-quality dark chocolate in a deep bowl. Let cool to room temperature. Dip each cookie, about halfway, into the chocolate and place on the baking sheet. Allow the cookies to set completely, about 45 minutes, before serving.

Lemon Make the recipe "as is" but add about 3 teaspoons of fresh lemon zest with the sugar. Orange zest works just as well.

Vanilla Bean Paste Make the recipe "as is" but add about 1 tablespoon of vanilla bean paste with the sugar and omit the fleur de sel. Other extracts (i.e., coffee, maple) can be substituted as well.

CHOCOLATE GINGER MOLASSES COOKIE

THIS VERSION OF THE CLASSIC GINGER MOLASSES COOKIE IS GIVEN A BAKED MAKEOVER, REPLETE WITH CHOCOLATE, LARGER THAN SHOULD BE ALLOWED, AND TOOTHSOME. I assure you it deserves a spot on your list of rotating recipes.

YIELD: ABOUT 36 COOKIES

MAKE THE MOLASSES COOKIES

In a medium bowl, whisk the flour with the cocoa powder, ginger, cinnamon, cloves, baking soda, baking powder, and salt. In the bowl of a standing electric mixer fitted with the paddle, beat the softened butter with the shortening at medium speed until the mixture is smooth, about 30 seconds. Add the sugar and beat until fluffy, about 2 minutes.

Add the egg to the cookie batter and beat until incorporated. Beat in the molasses and then the melted chocolate. Add the flour mixture in three batches, beating between additions. Divide the dough into three equal parts. Shape each part into a disk, then wrap each one in plastic wrap and refrigerate the cookie dough until chilled, about 2 hours.

Preheat the oven to 350 degrees F. Line two large baking sheets with parchment paper. On a lightly floured work surface, roll out one disk of dough ¼ inch thick. Using 4- to 5-inch cookie cutters, cut the dough into shapes and transfer to the prepared baking sheets. Reroll the dough scraps and cut out more cookies. Bake the cookies for about 7 minutes, rotating the pans halfway through the baking time until the tops are dry. Let the cookies cool on the pans for 5 minutes, then transfer to wire racks to cool completely. Repeat the process with the remaining dough.

MAKE THE ICING

In a medium bowl, combine the confectioners' sugar with the egg white and lemon juice and whisk until the icing is completely smooth. Scrape the icing into a piping bag fitted with a small tip. Decorate the cookies as desired. Let stand until the icing dries, about 30 minutes. Store tightly covered for 3 days.

Ingredients

FOR THE MOLASSES COOKIES

3¼ cups all-purpose flour, plus more for dusting

⅓ cup dark unsweetened cocoa powder (like Valrhona)

1 tablespoon ground ginger

2 teaspoons ground cinnamon

1 teaspoon ground cloves

1 tablespoon baking soda

½ teaspoon baking powder

1 teaspoon salt

5 tablespoons unsalted butter, softened

⅓ cup vegetable shortening

½ cup firmly packed dark brown sugar

1 large egg, at room temperature

½ cup molasses

2 ounces bittersweet chocolate, melted and cooled

FOR THE ICING

1¼ cups confectioners' sugar

1 large egg white

1 teaspoon fresh lemon juice

Ingredients

FOR THE COOKIES

4 cups all-purpose flour

¾ cup malt powder

2 teaspoons baking powder

½ teaspoon baking soda

½ teaspoon salt

1 cup (2 sticks) unsalted butter, at room temperature

1 cup firmly packed dark brown sugar

1 cup granulated sugar

2 eggs

⅓ cup sour cream

2 teaspoons pure vanilla extract

FOR THE VANILLA FILLING

5 ounces vegetable shortening, at room temperature

4 tablespoons (½ stick) unsalted butter, cut into small chunks, at room temperature

3¼ cups confectioners' sugar, sifted

½ teaspoon salt

1 tablespoon pure vanilla extract

1 teaspoon light rum

Baked Note

Keep a close eye on these cookies while they're baking—they go from chewy to crispy in a matter of minutes. The recipe instructions are written with a crispier cookie in mind—I prefer the crunch in contrast with the smoothness of the filling. But those who like their cookies on the chewier side can bake the cookies a few minutes shy of the suggested cooking time and pull them out before they start to crack on top.

MALTED MILK SANDWICH COOKIES

THERE IS A TREASURE TROVE OF A BOOKSTORE IN NEW YORK CITY CALLED BONNIE SLOT-NICK COOKBOOKS. It is a local bookshop filtered through a West Village lens: small, quaint, very knowledgeable staff of one, odd hours, well stocked. Better yet, it trades largely in vintage cookbooks. Luckily, Bonnie lets customers browse (though I always buy more than I need), and it was during such a session that I made an important discovery. Malt powder, one of my favorite ingredients, was a star in vintage cookbooks and was widely featured in the Pillsbury Bake-Off contenders for years. Malt powder was everywhere, and then it nearly disappeared. I am glad that a malt resurgence has recently taken hold, and I am equally pleased with this spin on the classic Oreo. If you are feeling exceedingly motivated, I suggest you make the Salt-n-Pepper Cookies at the same time you make these. They both contain the same filling (so you can just double it).

← YIELD: ABOUT 30 SANDWICH COOKIES →

MAKE THE COOKIES

In a large bowl, whisk together the flour, malt, baking powder, baking soda, and salt. Set aside.

In the bowl of a standing mixer fitted with the paddle attachment, beat the butter and sugars together until light and fluffy. Scrape down the bowl and add the eggs, one at a time, beating until each is incorporated. Add the sour cream and vanilla and beat until just incorporated. Add half of the dry ingredients all at once and beat for 15 seconds. Again, scrape down the bowl, then add the remaining dry ingredients and beat until just incorporated. The mixture should come together almost in a ball.

Loosely shape the dough into two balls, wrap them tightly in plastic wrap, and refrigerate for at least 3 hours.

Preheat the oven to 350 degrees F. Line two baking sheets with parchment paper.

Divide each dough ball in half, to make four portions. Place one portion on a lightly flour-dusted work surface and return the other three to the refrigerator.

Roll out the dough so that it is ¼ inch thick. The dough will be sticky, so you may have to flip and lightly flour it a few times while you work. Use a 2-inch round cookie cutter to create the sandwich tops and bottoms, and transfer them to the prepared baking sheets, leaving about 1 inch of space around each cookie. Extra dough scraps can be refrigerated and rerolled once more, if desired.

Bake the cookies for 10 to 12 minutes, or until they are just slightly browned. Place the baking sheets on wire racks to cool for 5 minutes. Use a spatula to transfer the cookies to the racks to cool completely.

While the cookies cool, prepare the filling.

MAKE THE VANILLA FILLING

In the bowl of a standing mixer fitted with the paddle attachment, beat the shortening and butter until lump free and smooth. Add the sugar in three parts, mixing each part until just combined. Add the salt, vanilla, and rum and beat again for 10 seconds. The filling should be thick but spreadable (like the inside of an Oreo). If it is too thick, add a drop or two of water as needed. Keep adding water to reach desired consistency, but do not add too much water or the filling will be too thin.

Alternatively if the mixture is too thin, add a few tablespoons of confectioners' sugar.

ASSEMBLE THE MALTED MILK SANDWICH COOKIES

Use a pastry bag or a small spoon to apply about 2 tablespoons of filling to the flat side of a cookie. Place another cookie, flat side down, on top. Press down slightly so that the filling spreads to the edges of the cookie. Repeat until all the sandwich cookies are made. Let them set up for about 15 minutes before serving. Store the cookies at room remperature in an airtight container for up to 3 days.

CHOCOLATE WHOOPIE PIES

LET'S FACE IT, THE CHOCOLATE WHOOPIE PIE IS OFFICIALLY A CLASSIC AMERICAN DESSERT.
I am the first person to admit that the term "classic" is overused, abused, and
on the verge of becoming meaningless; however, it would be a travesty not to
give this dessert its due. The whoopie pie, essentially two cake-like cookies
with a generous helping of a creamy filling sandwiched between them, has its
roots in the Northeast. Pennsylvanians will tell you they originated in Pennsylvania Dutch country, and the people of Maine will argue that it comes
from their state. This version features a very moist, deep-chocolate cookie
and a light and fluffy vanilla filling (for good measure, we also provide an
option for a peanut butter filling). Enjoy—and spread the whoopie religion. It
can become as ubiquitous as the chocolate chip cookie and the all-American
brownie with a little help from you.

YIELD: 10 TO 12 LARGE OR 15 TO 17 SMALL PIES

MAKE THE CHOCOLATE COOKIES

Preheat the oven to 350 degrees F. Line two baking sheets with parchment
paper.

In a large bowl, whisk together the flour, salt, baking powder, and baking
soda, and set aside.

In another large bowl, whisk together the cocoa powder and espresso powder.
Add the hot coffee and ½ cup hot water and whisk until both powders are
completely dissolved.

In a medium bowl, stir the brown sugar and oil together. Add this to the cocoa
mixture and whisk until combined. Add the egg, vanilla, and buttermilk and
whisk until smooth.

Use a rubber spatula to gently fold the dry ingredients into the wet ingredients. Make sure to scrape down the sides and bottom of the bowl as you fold.

Use a small ice cream scoop with a release mechanism to drop heaping tablespoons of the dough onto the prepared baking sheets about 1 inch apart. Bake
for 10 to 15 minutes, until the cookies are just starting to crack on top and a

toothpick inserted into the center of a cookie comes out clean. Let the cookies cool completely on the pan while you make the Swiss vanilla filling.

MAKE THE SWISS VANILLA FILLING

In a medium bowl, whisk the egg whites and sugar together (see note below and remember to substitute the sugar for the peanut butter filling variation). Set the bowl over a pan of simmering water but do not let the water touch the bottom of the bowl. Heat the mixture until the sugar is completely dissolved and the color is a milky white, about 2 to 3 minutes.

Transfer the egg mixture to the bowl of an electric mixer fitted with the whisk attachment and beat on medium-high speed (start slowly at first) until smooth and fluffy, about 5 minutes. Remove the whisk attachment and replace with the paddle attachment. Add the cubed butter and beat on medium-high speed (start slowly at first) until smooth and fluffy, about 5 minutes. If the buttercream looks like it is breaking, don't worry, it will eventually come together.

Add the salt and vanilla and beat for 5 seconds to combine.

✳ Peanut Butter Filling Variation: Replace the sugar with 1 cup granulated sugar and ½ cup light brown sugar (packed tightly). Fold in ¼ cup unsalted smooth peanut butter after adding the vanilla exract.

ASSEMBLE THE WHOOPIE PIES

Turn half of the cooled cookies upside down (flat side facing up).

Use an ice cream scoop or a tablespoon to drop a large dollop of filling onto the flat side of the cookie. Place another cookie, flat side down, on top of the filling. Press down slightly so that the filling spreads to the edges of the cookie. Repeat until all the cookies are used. Put the whoopie pies in the refrigerator for about 30 minutes to firm up before serving.

The whoopie pies will keep for up to 3 days, on a parchment-lined baking sheet covered with plastic wrap, in the refrigerator. Bring the whoopies to room temperature before serving.

BLACK AND WHITE COOKIES

I SPENT THE FIRST TWO YEARS OF MY TIME IN NEW YORK CITY LOOKING FOR THE PERFECT BLACK AND WHITE COOKIE. It was a mission bordering on obsession. The black and white cookie is nearly ubiquitous throughout the five boroughs, and there are many versions to be found in the various delis, bakeries, and even grocery stores. The black and white is, in my book, the official cookie of New York City. Though this honor is probably not recognized by any city agency, it is assumed, and that status is duly protected by the citizens. In fact, the merits of the various versions of the cookie are so heavily debated among devotees that we were nervous about supporting any one recipe. In the end, we went with a fairly straightforward adaptation: cakey vanilla cookie, thin layer of vanilla (white) frosting and thin layer of chocolate (black) frosting.

YIELD: 12 TO 18 COOKIES

MAKE THE COOKIES

Preheat the oven to 350 degrees F. Line two baking sheets with parchment paper.

In a large bowl, sift together the flour, baking soda, baking powder, and salt.

In the bowl of a standing mixer fitted with the paddle attachment, cream the butter and sugar until fluffy, about 2 minutes. Scrape down the bowl and add the eggs and egg yolk one at a time, beating briefly after each addition. Scrape down the sides and bottom of the bowl again, and mix on low speed for 10 seconds. Add the flour mixture in three parts, alternating with the buttermilk in two parts (end with the flour mixture). Scrape down the bowl; add the vanilla and lemon zest, and mix on low speed for a few more seconds.

Using a ¼-cup ice cream scoop, drop the dough onto the prepared baking sheets, leaving about 3 inches around each cookie. (You'll be able to fit about 6 cookies onto each sheet.)

Bake the cookies for about 17 minutes, rotating the sheets between the oven racks halfway through the baking time, until edges are golden brown and the

Ingredients

FOR THE COOKIE

3 cups all-purpose flour

½ teaspoon baking soda

½ teaspoon baking powder

½ teaspoon salt

14 tablespoons (1¾ sticks) unsalted butter, cool but not cold

1¼ cups granulated sugar

2 large eggs

1 large egg yolk

¾ cup buttermilk

1 tablespoon pure vanilla extract

1 tablespoon freshly grated lemon zest

FOR THE BLACK AND WHITE FROSTING

3¾ cups confectioners' sugar

4 to 5 tablespoons whole milk

3 tablespoons heavy cream

2 teaspoons pure vanilla extract

½ cup plus 2 tablespoons dark unsweetened cocoa powder (like Valrhona)

Baked Note

Icing a black and white cookie isn't difficult—a slightly messy decoration just screams "homemade," and that's not a terrible thing. However, if you are aiming for a perfectly iced cookie, fill a pastry bag fitted with a medium tip with the vanilla frosting, draw carefully defined outlines on half the cookie, then fill them in. Let the vanilla dry thoroughly and follow with the chocolate.

tops spring back when gently touched. Place the baking sheets on wire racks to cool for 5 minutes, then transfer the cookies to the racks to cool completely.

MAKE THE BLACK AND WHITE FROSTING

In a large bowl, whisk together the confectioners' sugar, milk, cream, and vanilla. If the mixture is too thick, add milk by the teaspoon until the desired consistency is reached. Pour half of the frosting (about ¾ cup) into a separate bowl and add the cocoa powder and 1 teaspoon water. Stir to incorporate the cocoa powder. The chocolate frosting should be about the same consistency as the "white" frosting. If it is too thick, keep adding water by the teaspoon until you get the right balance.

Use an offset spatula to spread white frosting on half of the flat side of each cookie. Let stand until almost set, about 20 minutes. Clean the spatula and use it to spread chocolate frosting over the unfrosted half of each cookie. (If the frosting thickens up while you are working, whisk it until it loosens.) Let the frosted cookies set completely, about 1 hour, before serving them.

Black and White Cookies are essentially little cakes, and they taste best eaten the day they are made. However, you can store them in an airtight container for up to 3 days at room temperature.

1¾ cups all-purpose flour

1 cup firmly packed dark brown sugar

½ teaspoon baking soda

1½ tablespoons cinnamon

½ teaspoon freshly grated nutmeg

½ teaspoon ground cloves

½ teaspoon ground ginger

½ teaspoon salt

10 tablespoons (1¼ sticks) butter, cool but not cold, cut into ½-inch cubes

1 egg, beaten

1 teaspoon freshly grated orange zest

Coarse sugar

Baked Note

During this absurdly fun cookie research, I ran into many cousins or relatives of speculaas. There are fluffier, anise-flavored versions from Germany and mass-produced, less-spiced versions known collectively as Dutch windmill cookies. The recipe printed here is as close to the Biscoff as it was possible to get.

SPECULAAS

THOSE DAMNED DELTA AIR LINES BISCOFF COOKIES HAUNT ME. I really hate flying, but I have to admit they are the one part of it that I enjoy. There are few cookies that I would pilfer in large quantities from a stewardess's mobile cart, but I would do almost anything to satiate my craving for those. They are actually speculaas, a type of Dutch or Belgian shortcrust biscuit. Traditionally served on St. Nicholas's Eve (December 6), speculaas are crunchy, golden, and chock-full of the traditional holiday spices: cinnamon, ginger, nutmeg, and cloves. They are also highly addictive and pair well with tea or coffee.

YIELD: ABOUT TWENTY-FOUR 2-INCH ROUND COOKIES

In a large bowl, whisk together the flour, brown sugar, baking soda, cinnamon, nutmeg, cloves, cardamom, ginger, and salt

Drop the butter over the flour mixture, and use a large fork or a pastry cutter to cut the butter into the flour until the mixture resembles coarse sand.

Add the beaten egg and orange zest, and cut the mixture again until just combined.

Use your hands to knead the dough (do not overwork it) until it forms a ball. The dough should be slightly sticky and break apart easily, but shouldn't stick to your hands. Cover it in plastic wrap and chill for at least 1 hour.

Preheat the oven to 350 degrees F. Line two baking sheets with parchment paper.

Unwrap and divide the chilled dough into two equal portions. Place one on a lightly flour-dusted work surface and return the other to the refrigerator.

Roll the dough into a ¼-inch-thick round. You may have to flip and lightly flour the dough a few times while rolling it out to keep it from sticking. Use any cookie cutter (a rectangular or oblong shape is the most traditional) to cut out the cookies, and transfer them to the prepared baking sheets, leaving about 1 inch of space around them. Extra dough scraps can be refrigerated and rerolled once more, if desired.

Sprinkle the tops of the cookies with coarse sugar. Bake the cookies for 15 minutes, rotating the baking sheets halfway through the baking time. The tops of the cookie should be just a bit dry and dark brown. Remove from the oven and place the baking sheets on wire racks to cool for 5 minutes. Use a spatula to transfer the cookies to the racks to cool completely.

Speculaas can be stored at room temperature, tightly covered, for up to 5 days.

A LITTLE BIT OF SUGAR

Thankfully, the sugar section of the local grocery store is growing. Offerings now include many organic, specialty, and alternative sugars and I urge you to experiment with them. In the interest of keeping things simple (and in the interest of saving precious kitchen space) I only use a few sugars in this book.

Coarse Sugar Larger grained sugar, perfect for decorating. Also known as pearl sugar.

Confectioners Sugar Commonly known as "icing," "10X," or "powdered" sugar, confectioners' sugar is often used to make frostings, icings, and whip cream. Confectioner's sugar contains a small amount of corn starch.

Dark Brown and Light Brown Sugar Brown sugar contains molasses (dark brown sugar contains more molasses than light brown sugar) and I use it with abandon.

Granulated Sugar This is the regular, omnipresent sugar. Lately, I have been playing with organic granulated sugar and have been extremely pleased with the results.

RED VELVET WHOOPIE PIES

RED VELVET CAKE, ONCE A MINOR CURIOSITY, IS NOW UBIQUITOUS IN AMERICAN BAKE-SHOPS. It is a trend that outlasted its trendiness. Though most closely identified as a Southern recipe, the red velvet probably originated somewhere in the Northeast as a cocoa powder- and buttermilk-based cake. In theory, the cocoa powder reacts with the baking soda to create a reddish hue, but somewhere along the way, the red quotient began to be upped with an unhealthy dose of red dye. Unfortunately, a rash of basic vanilla cakes containing buckets of red dye suddenly became "red velvet cakes." True red velvet needs at least three ingredients to qualify for the moniker: cocoa powder, buttermilk, and shortening (it lends a great fluffy texture). I include all of these in our Red Velvet Whoopie Pies, and fill them with a delectable cream cheese frosting. It is a Southern/Northern hybrid that looks great and tastes even better.

YIELD: 10 TO 12 LARGE OR 15 TO 17 SMALL PIES

MAKE THE PIES

Preheat the oven to 350 degrees F. Line two baking sheets with parchment paper.

In a large bowl, sift together the flour, cocoa powder, baking powder, baking soda, and salt.

In a small bowl, whisk together the canola oil and buttermilk.

In the bowl of an electric mixer fitted with the paddle attachment, cream the butter and shortening until smooth. Scrape down the bowl and add the sugars. Beat until the mixture is light and fluffy, about 5 minutes. Add the egg and vanilla extract and beat until combined. Scrape down the sides and bottom of the bowl, add the red gel food coloring, then mix on low speed for a few more seconds to incorporate. Do not overmix.

Turn the mixer to low. Add the flour mixture, alternating with the buttermilk mixture, in three separate additions, beginning and ending with the flour mix-

Ingredients

FOR THE WHOOPIE PIES

2½ cups all-purpose flour

3 tablespoons dark unsweetened cocoa powder (like Valrhona)

½ teaspoon baking powder

½ teaspoon baking soda

½ teaspoon salt

¼ cup canola oil

½ cup plus 2 tablespoons buttermilk

½ cup butter (1 stick), softened, cut into pieces

1 tablespoon vegetable shortening, at room temperature

¾ cup firmly packed dark brown sugar

¼ cup granulated sugar

1 large egg

1 teaspoon pure vanilla extract

1 tablespoon red gel food coloring

FOR THE CREAM CHEESE FILLING

3 cups confectioners' sugar

½ cup (1 stick) unsalted butter, softened

8 ounces cream cheese, softened

1 teaspoon pure vanilla extract

¼ teaspoon salt

FOR THE ASSEMBLY

½ cup toasted walnuts, chopped coarsely

ture until just combined. Scrape down the sides and bottom of the bowl, then mix on low speed for a few more seconds.

Cover with plastic wrap and chill the batter in the refrigerator for about 15 minutes.

Remove the batter from the refrigerator. Use a small ice cream scoop with a release mechanism to drop heaping tablespoons of the dough onto the prepared baking sheets about 1 inch apart. Bake for 10 to 20 minutes, until the cookies are just starting to crack on top and a toothpick inserted into the center of a cookie comes out clean. Let the cookies cool completely on the pan while you make the filling.

MAKE THE CREAM CHEESE FILLING

Sift the confectioners' sugar into a medium bowl and set aside.

In the bowl of an electric mixer fitted with the paddle attachment, beat the butter until is completely smooth. Add the cream creese and beat until combined.

Add the confectioners' sugar, vanilla, and salt and beat until smooth. Be careful not to overbeat the filling, or it will lose structure. (The filling can be made 1 day ahead. Cover the bowl tightly and put it in the refrigerator. Let the filling soften at room temperature before using).

ASSEMBLE THE WHOOPIE PIES

Spread the walnuts in an even layer on a small plate.

Turn half of the cooled cookies upside down (flat side facing up).

Use an ice cream scoop or a tablespoon to drop a large dollop of filling onto the flat side of the cookie. Place another cookie, flat side down, on top of the filling. Press down slightly so that the filling spreads to the edges of the cookie. Turn the whoopie on its side and roll through the walnuts. Repeat until all the cookies are used. Put the whoopie pies in the refrigerator for about 30 minutes to firm up before serving.

The whoopie pies will keep for up to 3 days on a parchment-lined baking sheet covered with plastic wrap, in the refrigerator.

PEANUT BUTTER AND JELLY BARS

THE PEANUT BUTTER AND JELLY BAR IS, OF COURSE, A NOD TO THE MOST FAMOUS OF LUNCH-BOX SANDWICHES. It is a playful take (playful without being silly) on an iconic American flavor pairing. If you are a PB and J fan, I urge you to give these a try. They have been a staple of the Baked menu since opening day, and are among our most popular snack items. The heaps of peanut butter and mounds of jelly are sandwiched between a sweet crust and chunky crumble. It's a bit of a picnic dessert. Or the perfect lunch substitute.

YIELD: 15 LARGE BARS

MAKE THE SWEET PASTRY DOUGH

Butter the sides and bottom of a glass or light-colored metal 9-by-13-inch pan. Line the bottom with a sheet of parchment paper, and butter the parchment. Put the sugar, flour, and salt in a food processor and pulse until combined. Add the butter and pulse until sandy (about 6 to 10 quick pulses). In a small bowl, whisk the eggs and pour them into the food processor. Pulse just until the dough begins to hold together. Form the dough into a disk, wrap it tightly in plastic, and refrigerate for at least 1 hour or overnight.

Dust a work surface with a sprinkling of flour. Using a rolling pin, roll the dough into a rectangle slightly larger than 9 by 13 inches (the size of the pan) and about ¼ inch thick. (The dough might be sticky. Make sure to turn it with a bench knife or offset spatula as needed and keep the working surface floured. Some people find it easier to roll the dough between two layers of parchment paper. This can make it easier to transfer and be a bit less messy.)

Ever so gently, guide the dough into the pan and lightly press it—without pulling—into the bottom; it is not necessary to bring the dough up the sides of the pan, only to completely cover the bottom of the pan. Trim off any excess. Place the pan in the freezer for 30 minutes.

Preheat the oven to 375 degrees F.

Remove the pan from the freezer, line it with aluminum foil, and fill it three-

Ingredients

FOR THE SWEET PASTRY DOUGH

¼ cup granulated sugar

1½ cups all-purpose flour

¼ teaspoon salt

½ cup (1 stick) cold unsalted butter, cut into ½-inch cubes

1 large egg

FOR THE PEANUT BUTTER FILLING

1 cup (2 sticks) unsalted butter, at room temperature

2 cups smooth peanut butter or 1 cup smooth peanut butter and 1 cup chunky peanut butter

1¾ cups confectioners' sugar

½ teaspoon pure vanilla extract

FOR THE CRUMB TOPPING

¾ cups all-purpose flour

¼ teaspoon salt

½ teaspoon baking powder

¼ teaspoon baking soda

¼ teaspoon cinnamon

⅓ cup firmly packed dark brown sugar

⅔ cup rolled oats

6 tablespoons (¾ stick) cold unsalted butter, cut into ½-inch pieces

FOR THE ASSEMBLY

2 heaping cups good-quality jelly or preserves

Baked Note

This is a rare peanut-butter flavored dessert for which you can easily replace the smooth peanut butter with a chunkier variety in equal parts. I almost always make the bars with grape jelly, but feel free to use your favorite preserves.

quarters full with pie weights or dried beans. Bake for 15 minutes, then remove the foil and weights and bake for another 10 minutes, or until the crust is lightly browned. Transfer the pan to a wire rack to cool.

Reduce the oven temperature to 325 degrees F.

MAKE THE PEANUT BUTTER FILLING

In the bowl of a standing mixer fitted with the paddle attachment, beat the butter until it is completely smooth. Add the peanut butter and beat until combined. Add the confectioners' sugar and vanilla and beat until smooth. Scrape down the sides of the bowl and beat again. Turn the mixture out onto the crust and, using an offset spatula, spread it into an even layer. Chill the peanut butter layer while you make the crumb topping.

MAKE THE CRUMB TOPPING

In a large bowl, whisk together the flour, baking powder, salt, baking soda, and cinnamon. Add the brown sugar and use your hands to rub it in until the mixture is uniform in color. Stir in the oats.

Place the dry mix in the bowl of a standing mixer fitted with the paddle attachment. Add the butter and beat on low speed until loose crumbs form.

TO ASSEMBLE THE BARS

Spread the jelly in an even layer over the peanut butter filling. Sprinkle on the crumb topping until the jelly is no longer visible.

Bake the bars for 20 to 25 minutes, rotating the pan halfway through, or until the top is brown.

Transfer the pan to a wire rack to cool completely, then cut the bars and serve.

The bars can be stored in the refrigerator in an airtight container for up to 2 days.

ROSEMARY APRICOT SQUARES

I AM, AND ALWAYS WILL BE, A DESSERT PURIST. I prefer my desserts fuss free, full of chocolate, and usually accompanied by a side of vanilla ice cream. I shy away from forced savory/sweet combinations and headline grabbers (bacon cupcakes, anyone?)—but I will make and try anything at least once. Usually, I then retreat to a peanut butter–chocolate default. So I was a little bit surprised by how hard I fell for these bars. Our Rosemary Apricot Squares are the creation of Eric Wolitzky and Patrick Panella, two rising talents in the baking world (coincidentally, they put some time in at Baked). The moment they presented them to me, I added them to our regular menu rotation. The rosemary short dough is light and elegant without being overpowering, and it combines well with the not-so-sweet apricot filling. They are great for breakfast, afternoon coffee, and casual dinners. In short, they are my chocolate-alternative dessert. If there has to be such a thing.

YIELD: 9 LARGE BARS

MAKE THE ROSEMARY SHORT DOUGH

Lightly spray a 9-inch square baking pan with nonstick cooking spray and line it with parchment paper, allowing the parchment to just overhang on two sides.

In a medium bowl, whisk together the flour, salt, and rosemary. In the bowl of a standing mixer fitted with the paddle attachment, beat the butter with the confectioners' sugar and vanilla at medium speed until fluffy, approximately 2 minutes. Turn the mixer to the lowest speed and stream in the flour mixture. Scrape the dough into the prepared pan, lightly flour your clean hands, and press it into an even layer. Place the pan in the refrigerator for at least 30 minutes.

Preheat the oven to 350 degrees F.

Bake the short crust until it is golden, 25 to 30 minutes, rotating the pan halfway through the baking time. Cool the pan on a wire rack. Leave the oven on.

Ingredients

FOR THE ROSEMARY SHORT DOUGH

1¾ cups all-purpose flour

½ teaspoon salt

2½ teaspoons fresh rosemary leaves, minced

12 tablespoons (1½ sticks) unsalted butter, cut into ½-inch cubes, at room temperature

½ cup confectioners' sugar, sifted

¾ teaspoon pure vanilla extract

FOR THE APRICOT FILLING

2 cups dried California apricots (about 8½ ounces)

½ cup granulated sugar

3 tablespoons honey

2 tablespoons brandy

Pinch salt

FOR THE CRUMB TOPPING

½ cup all-purpose flour

½ cup firmly packed dark brown sugar

⅓ cup pecans, coarsely chopped

Pinch salt

3 tablespoons cold unsalted butter, cut into ½-inch cubes

Baked Note

I am hesitant to become your go-to source of apricot info, but here are a few personal notes: First, I always buy unsulfured apricots; the sulfured ones seem one step away from a freaky science experiment. Second, generally speaking, I find California apricots are tangier and have a stronger apricot flavor than some of their Middle Eastern counterparts.

MAKE THE APRICOT FILLING

Place the apricots, sugar, honey, brandy, and salt in a medium saucepan with 1½ cups water and simmer over low heat for 40 to 50 minutes, or until the apricots are fork-tender and most of the liquid has evaporated or thickened. Remove the pan from the heat and stir the mixture to release excess steam. Scrape the apricot mixture into a food processor and puree until smooth.

MAKE THE CRUMB TOPPING

In the bowl of a standing mixer fitted with the paddle attachment, combine the flour, brown sugar, pecans, and salt. Mix on low speed for 15 seconds. Add the butter and mix until a sandy crumb begins to form, about 1 minute. (At this point, the crumb topping can be stored, covered, in the refrigerator until ready to use).

ASSEMBLE THE ROSEMARY APRICOT SQUARES

Spread the apricot filling over the shortbread, then sprinkle the crumb topping over the filling. Bake for 20 to 25 minutes, or until the crumb has browned. Let the pastry cool for at least 30 minutes in the pan, then lift it out using the parchment paper overhang and cut it into bars. The bars can be stored in refrigerator, tightly wrapped, for up to 3 days.

Ingredients

FOR THE GRAHAM CRUST

2 cups crushed graham cracker crumbs

1 tablespoon firmly packed dark brown sugar

½ teaspoon salt

10 tablespoons (1¼ sticks) unsalted butter, melted

FOR THE CHOCOLATE PUDDING FILLING

4 ounces good-quality dark chocolate (60 to 72%), coarsely chopped

3 tablespoons cornstarch

¾ cup granulated sugar

6 egg yolks

1 teaspoon pure vanilla extract

2 cups whole milk

½ cup heavy cream

2 tablespoons whiskey

Simple Whipped Cream for serving (optional, page 159)

Dark cocoa powder (like Valrhona) for serving (optional)

Baked Note

These pudding bars work well as pudding cups too. Simply press the graham crust into the bottom and up the sides of a 12-cup muffin pan, then bake and fill them as directed. Use an offset spatula to remove the individual cups and serve immediately.

AUNT SABRA KING'S PUDDING BARS

BLAIR VAN SANT, OUR FORMER PASTRY CHEF AND KITCHEN MANAGER EXTRAORDINAIRE, WAS ALSO OUR RESIDENT PUDDING EXPERT. He has since returned to the South, but he remains a close friend and an avid pudding freak. In the service of this book, I asked him to dig up his oldest pudding inspiration. Blair got back to me in twenty-six seconds flat. Aunt Sabra King's Pudding Bar is a messy Sunday supper–style dessert that epitomizes the beauty of Southern baking: not too fussy, very rich, and slightly boozy. Aunt Sabra herself is a gin-drinking, card-playing, silver Cadillac–driving lady. The exact origin of this recipe is unknown, but Aunt Sabra King (through a variety of inspired tweaks and nods) made it her very own.

YIELD: 24 BARS

MAKE THE GRAHAM CRUST

Preheat the oven to 325 degrees F.

In a medium bowl, stir together the graham cracker crumbs, brown sugar, and salt. Pour the butter over the crumb mixture and stir until well combined. The mixture will feel wet. Turn the crumb mixture out into a 9-by-13-inch pan and press it into the bottom and up the sides. Use the back of a large spoon to get an even layer. Place the crust in the refrigerator for 30 minutes.

Bake the crust for approximately 10 minutes, or until it is golden brown. Set it on a wire rack to cool while you make the filling.

MAKE THE CHOCOLATE PUDDING FILLING

Place the chocolate in a medium heatproof bowl and set it aside.

In a large, heatproof bowl, whisk together the cornstarch and ½ cup of the sugar. Add the egg yolks and whisk until combined. Add the vanilla and whisk again.

In a medium saucepan over medium heat, whisk together the milk, cream, and the remaining ¼ cup sugar. Bring the mixture just to a boil. Add a third of the hot milk mixture to the egg mixture, whisking constantly. Keep whisking the egg mixture and add another third of the hot milk mixture. Transfer the egg mixture into the saucepan with the milk mixture and, whisking constantly, bring it to a boil over medium-high heat. Boil for 2 to 3 minutes, or until the pudding is very thick.

Remove the pan from the heat and strain the mixture through a fine-mesh sieve directly onto the chocolate. Stir until it is smooth. Add the whiskey and stir again.

ASSEMBLE THE PUDDING BARS

Let the pudding mixture cool for about 20 minutes. Whisk it one more time until it is smooth and pour it over the cooled graham crust. Spread the pudding into an even layer. Cover it with plastic wrap and refrigerate for at least 4 hours.

Cut into squares and serve with whipped cream and a sprinkling of cocoa, if desired.

The bars can be stored, tightly covered, in the refrigerator for up to 2 days.

JOE FROGGERS,
OR GINGER RUM MOLASSES COOKIES

I HAD ACTUALLY NEVER HEARD OF THE JOE FROGGER UNTIL I STUMBLED UPON A BAKERY IN MAINE SELLING THESE COOKIES BY THE DOZEN. They were huge—each one the size of a small pancake—and utterly addictive. Though I found the Joe Frogger in Maine, it is a native of Marblehead, Massachusetts, named after a famous resident, Joe Brown. In short, "Uncle Joe" supposedly baked these molasses-heavy cookies by the dozens for the fishermen and denizens of Marblehead, and he sold them at his tavern on Gingerbread Hill (how fitting!). Regardless of the historical origins of the Joe Frogger, I am a fan. The molasses and dark rum blend perfectly, and it has a likeable chewy snap.

YIELD: 36 TO 48 COOKIES, DEPENDING ON SIZE OF THE CUTTER

Whisk the flour, salt, ginger, nutmeg, cloves, and baking soda together. Set aside.

In the bowl of a standing mixer fitted with the paddle attachment, beat the butter and shortening together until there are no visible lumps. Add both sugars and beat just until incorporated. Scrape down the bowl, add the molasses, and beat until the mixture is uniform in color.

Prepare ⅓ cup very hot water. Add the flour mixture to the butter mixture, alternating with the hot water, in three parts, beginning and ending with the flour mixture. Scrape down the bowl, add the rum, and mix for 15 seconds. Cover the bowl and chill for at least 3 hours or overnight.

Preheat the oven to 375 degrees F. Line two baking sheets with parchment paper. Dust a work surface with a sprinkling of flour. Roll the dough into a ¼-inch thick round. Cut out the cookies with a 2- to 3-inch round cookie cutter, and transfer them to the prepared baking sheets. Sprinkle a tiny bit of sanding sugar onto each cookie.

Bake the cookies for 8 to 12 minutes, until they are set. Place the baking sheet on a wire rack to cool for 5 minutes. Use a spatula to transfer the cookies to the rack to cool completely. Store in an airtight container for up to 3 days.

Ingredients

4 cups all-purpose flour

1½ teaspoons salt

1½ teaspoons ground ginger

½ teaspoon freshly grated nutmeg

½ teaspoon ground cloves

1 teaspoon baking soda

4 tablespoons (½ stick) unsalted butter

¼ cup vegetable shortening

¾ cup firmly packed dark brown sugar

¼ cup granulated sugar

1¼ cups molasses

3 tablespoons dark rum

Coarse sugar for decor

Baked Note

The original Joe Frogger uses vegetable shortening exclusively. I adapted the recipe to include some butter, but it would be a mistake to take out the shortening entirely. An all-butter cookie, while tasty, will spread more and won't retain the same bite over time. In other words, an all-butter cookie would not be a Joe Frogger, and that would be a shame. If you prefer a chewy cookie, bake for 8 minutes; if you like a crispier cookie, err on the 12-minute side.

CAKES

My cake patience is wearing thin. I can no longer pretend to be enthralled with a cake that is not really a cake. If it's in the shape of a designer shoe or is a lifelike replica of a favorite pet, it is really less about the cake and more about the design. It is form over function, cake as afterthought. This does not happen to other foods. I have yet to attend a party where the chef has sewn together a string of delicious steaks into a golf club or fedora. I have never seen (and hope to never see) a baby rattle composed of salmon fillets. But cake abuse has no limits. I admire the design and architecture involved to create these stunning showstoppers, but they are, too often, not something I would want to eat.

I am still a cake pusher. I adamantly believe that cake is the great centerpiece dessert for any affair, however ordinary—not just birthdays, graduations, and holidays. Too often, we relegate cake (primarily layer cake) to event status, but I like to serve it just for its own sake. I am too impatient to wait for the next wedding, or birthday, or engagement, or holiday.

While rummaging about old recipes and dusty cookbooks, I discovered a surprising thing about cakes. They haven't really changed much. I have a recipe for a chocolate cake that is at least forty years old, and it is probably no different from something you would find in the pages of today's food magazines. The methodology might be slightly different. The newer recipes, including ours, are written for standing mixers and other gadgets like food processors and mini grinders, while the older ones were geared toward elbow grease—centered techniques. Also, instructions are becoming more and more precise and increasingly lengthy. For better or worse, recipes went from being a quick paragraph to many paragraphs to a page or two. I am unsure about how to stop this predicament, as I am part of the problem. In just one instance, I transcribed my grandmother's favorite apple cake recipe from a small index card. After interpreting her shorthand and adding a few precise instructions, the recipe magically grew to two pages. I can't help myself.

The cakes in this chapter were culled to include a range representing every aspect of American baking. Of course we have the beloved cupcake, America's current reigning dessert champion, smartly symbolized by our wonderful Maple Cupcakes with Maple Cream Cheese Frosting (see page 160). My personal favorite, Burnt Sugar Bundt Cake, (see page 141) is everything a Bundt cake should be: tasty, hearty, and a great accompaniment to any meal, even breakfast. Then, of course, we included an array of stunning three-layer cakes. You should try them all, especially the Chocolate Coffee Cake with Dark Chocolate Ganache (see page 151). Actually, we hope you have a chance to work your way through each and every cake. We did, and we survived.

DEVIL'S FOOD CAKE
WITH ANGEL FROSTING

THE ORIGINS OF THE TERM "DEVIL'S FOOD" TO DESCRIBE CHOCOLATE CAKE ARE EXTREMELY DIFFICULT, IF NOT IMPOSSIBLE, TO IDENTIFY. However, even a cursory investigation shows that devil's food cake recipes started to appear at least as early as the 1920s. The recipes all vary slightly. There are versions with heaps of cinnamon, versions including a variety of nuts, and quite a few with mashed potatoes. In the end, however, devil's food cake is really just a chocolate cake that's more chocolaty than most. This cake is dense and moist without being heavy, and it's full of a rich chocolate flavor imparted by the combination of dark chocolate, dark cocoa powder, and coffee.

It is in my nature to cover any and every chocolate cake in a thick chocolate frosting, but I rather love the contrasting flavor of this fluffy, white Angel frosting. It is worth noting that this recipe makes a great cupcake. If you are adapting it for cupcake use, be sure to reduce the baking time by 25 minutes, keep a watchful eye on the oven, and only fill the cup holders three-quarters of the way full.

YIELD: ONE 8-INCH, 2-LAYER CAKE

MAKE THE DEVIL'S FOOD CAKE

Preheat the oven to 325 degrees F. Butter two 8-inch round cake pans, line the bottoms with parchment paper, and butter the parchment. Dust the parchment with flour and knock out the excess flour.

Place the chocolate and cocoa powder in a medium heatproof bowl. Pour the hot coffee directly over them and whisk until combined. Add the milk and whisk until smooth.

In another bowl, sift together the flour, baking soda, and salt. Set aside.

In the bowl of a standing mixer fitted with the paddle attachment, beat the butter and sugars on medium speed until fluffy, about 3 minutes. Add the eggs, one at a time, beating well after each addition, then add the vanilla and beat until incorporated. Scrape down the bowl and mix again for 30 seconds.

Ingredients

FOR THE DEVIL'S FOOD CAKE

1 ounce good-quality dark chocolate (60 to 72%), broken into a few pieces

½ cup dark unsweetened cocoa powder (like Valrhona)

⅔ cup hot coffee

⅓ cup whole milk

1⅓ cups all-purpose flour

1 teaspoon baking soda

½ teaspoon salt

10 tablespoons (1¼ sticks) unsalted butter, cut into ½-inch cubes, softened

1 cup firmly packed dark brown sugar

½ cup granulated sugar

3 large eggs

1 teaspoon pure vanilla extract

FOR THE ANGEL FROSTING

5 large egg whites, at room temperature

1½ cups granulated sugar

1 tablespoon light corn syrup

1 teaspoon vanilla paste (or 1½ teaspoons pure vanilla extract)

Baked Note

Even though this recipe uses almost an entire cup of hot coffee, the taste is undetectable in the final dessert. The coffee merely enhances the chocolate flavor while cutting a little bit of the sweetness. If you want, you can substitute the coffee for 2 teaspoons of instant espresso powder dissolved in ⅔ cup boiling water.

Add the flour mixture in three parts, alternating with the chocolate mixture, beginning and ending with the flour mixture.

Divide the batter into the prepared pans and smooth the tops. Bake for 35 to 40 minutes, rotating the pans halfway through the baking time, until a toothpick inserted in the center of the cake comes out clean. Transfer the pans to a wire rack and let cool for 45 minutes. Turn the cakes out onto the rack and let them cool completely. Remove the parchment.

MAKE THE ANGEL FROSTING

Place the egg whites in the bowl of a standing mixer fitted with the whisk attachment. Set aside.

In a medium saucepan over low heat, stir together 1¼ cups of the sugar, the corn syrup, and ¼ cup water. Once the sugar is dissolved, increase the heat to medium-high, and clip a candy thermometer onto the side of the pot. Heat the mixture, without stirring, to almost soft-ball stage (about 235 degrees F)—do not let it go above 235 degrees F.

While you wait for the syrup to reach the soft-ball stage, whip the egg whites on medium speed until soft peaks form—do not beat beyond this.

As soon as the sugar mixture reaches the soft-ball stage, remove the pan from the heat.

Sprinkle the remaining ¼ cup sugar over the soft peaks of the egg whites and turn the mixer to low. Slowly stream in the hot sugar syrup. Once all the syrup has been added, increase the speed to medium-high and beat the icing for about 7 minutes until it is thick and shiny. Add the vanilla and beat again for 10 seconds.

TO ASSEMBLE THE DEVIL'S FOOD CAKE

Place one cake layer on a serving platter. Trim the top to create a flat surface and evenly spread about 1 cup frosting on top. Place the next layer on top, then trim and frost it the same way. Frost the sides of the cake with the remaining frosting. Serve immediately.

Angel frosting tastes best if it is served within 4 hours of being made.

BOSTON CREAM PIE CAKE

AMAZINGLY, SOME DESSERTS—REALLY GREAT AMERICAN DESSERTS—ENTER THE AMERI-
CAN CONSCIOUSNESS, LINGER FOR YEARS, AND SLOWLY DISAPPEAR. For some reason,
they never reach icon or classic status. They become unfashionable or, even
worse, caricatures of their former selves. This has been the fate of the once-
beloved Boston cream pie. It used to be ubiquitous on dessert menus, in diner
cases, and even at the odd birthday party. My theories for its disappearance
are many, but mainly I blame the inadequate (or bad) versions that started
to appear throughout the country. A poorly executed Boston cream pie is one
bad dessert. There is nothing worse than fake pastry cream or an over-spongy
sponge.

Our Boston Cream Pie Cake is a tribute and an homage. We tweaked the
original to make a four-layer beast with all the important parts intact: a
bouncy milk sponge, classic vanilla and chocolate pastry cream, and a gooey
chocolate glaze. Messy? Yes. Good? Absolutely.

YIELD: ONE 8-INCH, 4-LAYER ROUND CAKE

MAKE THE MILK SPONGE CAKE

Preheat the oven to 325 degrees F. Butter two 8-inch round cake pans, line the
bottoms with parchment paper, and butter the parchment. Dust the parchment with flour and knock out the excess flour.

In a large bowl, sift the cake flour, baking powder, and salt together. Set aside.

In a small saucepan over low heat, stir together the butter and milk until the
butter is just melted. Do not overheat. Remove the pan from the heat and
set aside.

In the bowl of a standing mixer fitted with the whisk attachment, beat the
eggs, sugar, and vanilla on medium speed until the mixture is pale and has
tripled in volume, about 5 minutes.

Remove the bowl from the standing mixer and sprinkle a third of the flour
mixture over the egg mixture. Gently fold the two together, using a rubber
spatula. Add the rest of the flour mixture and fold again.

Ingredients

FOR THE MILK SPONGE CAKE

1¾ cups cake flour

1½ teaspoons baking powder

¾ teaspoon salt

6 tablespoons (¾ stick) unsalted butter, cut
into small pieces

¾ cup whole milk

4 large eggs

1¼ cups sugar

1½ teaspoons pure vanilla extract

FOR THE PASTRY CREAM FILLING

7 large egg yolks

¾ cup sugar

¼ teaspoon salt

⅓ cup cornstarch

3 cups whole milk

3 tablespoons unsalted butter

1 tablespoon pure vanilla extract

2 tablespoons light rum

6 ounces good-quality dark chocolate
(60 to 72%), finely chopped

FOR THE CHOCOLATE GLAZE

5 ounces good-quality dark chocolate
(60 to 72%), coarsely chopped

2 tablespoons dark unsweetened
cocoa powder (like Valrhona)

¼ cup sugar

¼ cup heavy cream

¼ cup light corn syrup

Pinch salt

½ teaspoon pure vanilla extract

1½ tablespoons unsalted butter

Add the warm milk mixture (if it has cooled completely, reheat it slightly) to the batter and gently fold until just incorporated.

Divide the batter between the prepared pans and smooth the tops. Bake for 20 to 25 minutes, rotating the pans halfway through the baking time, until a toothpick inserted in the center comes out clean. The cake might appear wobbly if you shake the pan, but if pressed gently in the middle, it should spring back.

Transfer the cake pans to a wire rack and let cool for 20 minutes. Turn the cakes out onto the rack and let them cool completely. Remove the parchment.

MAKE THE PASTRY CREAM FILLING

In a large bowl, whisk together the egg yolks, half of the sugar, the salt, and cornstarch until the mixture is pale, thick, and smooth.

In a medium saucepan over medium heat, stir together the milk and the remaining half of the sugar. Continue stirring until the mixture boils. Remove the pan from the heat, and pour about a third of the liquid into the egg mixture, whisking constantly. Transfer the tempered egg mixture back to the saucepan with the remaining milk mixture and, whisking constantly, bring to a boil over medium-high heat. Boil for 2 minutes.

Remove the pan from the heat and strain through a fine-mesh sieve into a large bowl. Stir in the butter, vanilla, and rum until combined.

Scoop a third of the pastry cream into a different bowl and set it aside. Add the chocolate to the warm pastry cream remaining in the pan and stir until melted and smooth. Scoop the chocolate cream into a bowl. Once both pastry creams have cooled for about 15 minutes, wrap both bowls in plastic wrap, pressing the plastic directly onto the top of the cream to prevent a skin from forming. Refrigerate until firm, about 4 hours or overnight.

MAKE THE CHOCOLATE GLAZE

Place the chocolate and cocoa powder in a large bowl and set it over a saucepan of simmering water, stirring occasionally, until completely melted and smooth.

In another small saucepan, combine the sugar, cream, corn syrup, and salt with ¼ cup water. Place the pan over low heat and warm, without stirring, until the sugar dissolves. Increase the heat to medium and simmer for about

4 minutes, stirring frequently. Remove the pan from the heat and whisk in the vanilla and butter. Whisk to release excess heat, then add the reserved chocolate mixture and stir until smooth. Set the sauce aside; it will thicken while you assemble the cake.

ASSEMBLE THE BOSTON CREAM PIE CAKE

Using a serrated knife, cut the cake layers in half horizontally. Place the first cake layer on a platter and scoop half of the chocolate pastry cream on top. Spread the cream evenly to the cake's edges using an offset spatula. Add a second cake layer and cover that with all the vanilla cream. Add a third cake layer and cover it with the remaining chocolate cream. Place the last cake layer on top and press gently with your palms to help the cake layers adhere to the pastry cream.

Very slowly, pour the thickened chocolate glaze onto the center of the top of the cake. Use an offset spatula to spread it out to the edges so that it drips down the sides of the cake. Let the sauce thicken for about 20 minutes before serving.

The cake tastes best when eaten within 24 hours. If you have leftovers, tent the entire cake in foil and refrigerate. Serve it chilled or at room temperature.

Baked Notes

Generally speaking, it is easier (though not necessary) to trim cake layers when they are frozen. If you have the time to bake your cake layers the day before you need to serve the dessert, simply wrap the cooled cake twice in plastic and place it in the freezer.

One more thing: I really like this cake with a rum soak. If the idea appeals to you, give it a try: First, use a toothpick and poke a few holes in the sponge after it cools from baking. Then heat 1 part sugar with 2 parts water until the sugar is dissolved. Add some rum (about 1 tablespoon) and brush the syrup over the layers before assembling the cake.

CARAMEL APPLE CAKE

PEOPLE IN UPSTATE NEW YORK ARE ABSOLUTELY WILD ABOUT THEIR APPLES. It's a wildness bordering on religious conviction, and they can rattle off the differences in varieties, which apples work best for which recipes, and how many acres of orchards have been lost to development. They also feel a sense of ownership of all things apple, even though New York does not hold the title of largest apple-producing state (that would go to Washington). Unsurprisingly, there are many variations on apple cake floating about the Northeast, each with a particular family-inflected nuance. Our version is hearty. It is moist, dense, lightly spiced, and covered in a slightly sweet caramel frosting that gives the cake a homey county-fair feel. This cake is pure fall. It is dedicated to the apple lovers of New York, and I can say for certain that I have never made it before August or after January.

YIELD: ONE 8-INCH, 3-LAYER CAKE

MAKE THE APPLE CAKE

Preheat the oven to 325 degrees F. Butter three 8-inch round cake pans, line the bottoms with parchment paper, and butter the parchment. Dust the parchment with flour and knock out the excess flour.

Sift the flour, baking soda, baking powder, salt, cinnamon, allspice, and cloves together into a large bowl. Set aside.

In the bowl of a standing mixer fitted with the paddle attachment, beat the butter until creamy, about 4 minutes. Add the sugar and beat until light and fluffy, about 3 minutes. Add the egg and beat until combined.

Add the flour mixture to the mixer bowl in three parts, alternating with the applesauce, beginning and ending with the flour mixture. Scrape down the bowl, then mix on low speed for a few more seconds.

Divide the batter among the prepared pans and smooth the tops. Bake for 40 to 45 minutes, rotating the pans halfway through the baking time, until a toothpick inserted in the center of the cake comes out clean. Transfer the pans to a wire rack and cool for 20 minutes. Turn the cakes out onto the rack, remove the parchment, and let cool completely.

MAKE THE CARAMEL BUTTERCREAM

In a medium, heavy-bottomed saucepan, whisk the sugar and flour together. Add the milk and cream and cook over medium heat, whisking occasionally, until the mixture comes to a boil and has thickened, about 10 to 15 minutes.

Transfer the mixture to the bowl of a standing mixer fitted with the paddle attachment. Beat on high speed until cool. Reduce the speed to low and add the butter and vanilla; mix until thoroughly incorporated. Increase the speed to medium-high and beat until the frosting is light and fluffy.

Add ⅓ cup of the caramel and continue mixing until combined. If the frosting is too soft, put the bowl in the refrigerator to chill slightly, then beat again until it is the proper consistency. If the frosting is too firm, set the bowl over a pot of simmering water and beat with a wooden spoon until it is the proper consistency.

ASSEMBLE THE CARAMEL APPLE CAKE

Place one cake layer on a serving platter. Trim the top to create a flat surface and evenly spread about 1¼ cups of the frosting on top. Add the next layer, trim and frost it, then add the third layer. Spread a very thin layer of frosting over the sides and top of the cake and put it in the refrigerator for about 15 minutes to firm up. (This is known as crumb coating and will help to keep loose cake crumbs under control when you frost the outside of the cake.) Frost the sides and top with the remaining frosting. Drizzle on a few swirls of caramel and refrigerate the finished cake for 15 minutes to firm it up before serving.

This cake will keep beautifully in a cake saver at room temperature for up to 3 days, as long as the weather is cool and humidity free. Otherwise, place the cake in a cake saver and refrigerate it for up to 3 days. Let a chilled cake sit at room temperature for at least 2 hours before serving.

BURNT SUGAR BUNDT CAKE
WITH CARAMEL RUM FROSTING

I AM ALL ABOUT BUNDT CAKES. IN FACT, TRUTH BE TOLD, I PREFER MAKING BUNDT CAKES TO JUST ABOUT ANYTHING. Bundts generally have a heartier feel and they are much easier to assemble than the classic three-layer cake. They travel well, and they keep like a dream. This Burnt Sugar Bundt Cake is loosely based on of one of those amazing cakes you find in a church supper cookbook and end up making over and over again. The burnt sugar adds a nice caramel flavor, and the coconut milk gives the cake a terrific moist crumb.

YIELD: ONE 10-INCH BUNDT CAKE

MAKE THE BURNT SUGAR LIQUID

In a medium saucepan over medium heat, slowly melt the sugar. Use a wooden spoon to stir it continuously to ensure even melting. When the sugar turns a dark caramel color, remove the pan from the heat and slowly stream in the cream while continuing to stir (don't worry if mixture starts to clump). Return the pan to medium heat and stir until completely combined; cook for 2 minutes longer, stirring.

Transfer the burnt caramel mixture to at least a 2-cup heatproof liquid measuring cup (like Pyrex) and add enough coconut milk to make 1¼ cups liquid. Add the lemon juice. Whisk to combine, divide the mixture in half, and set both portions aside.

MAKE THE BUNDT CAKE

Preheat the oven to 325 degrees F. Generously spray the inside of a 10-inch Bundt pan with nonstick cooking spray; alternatively, butter it thoroughly, dust it with flour, and knock out the excess flour.

In a medium bowl, whisk together the flour, baking powder, baking soda, and salt. Set aside.

In the bowl of a standing mixer fitted with the paddle attachment, beat the butter and sugar until pale and fluffy. Scrape down the bowl and add the eggs,

Ingredients

FOR THE BURNT SUGAR LIQUID

½ cup granulated sugar

½ cup heavy cream

Approximately ¾ cup coconut milk

1½ tablespoons fresh lemon juice

FOR THE BUNDT CAKE

3 cups all-purpose flour

1 teaspoon baking powder

½ teaspoon baking soda

1 teaspoon salt

1¼ cups unsalted butter (2½ sticks) cut into 1-inch cubes, at room temperature

2 cups granulated sugar

4 large eggs

1 teaspoon pure vanilla extract

Burnt Sugar Liquid (see above)

FOR THE CARAMEL RUM FROSTING

½ cup (1 stick) unsalted butter

2 tablespoons dark rum

2⅓ cups confectioners' sugar

Burnt Sugar Liquid (see above)

Baked Note

The frosting on this cake is very versatile. If you want to omit the alcohol, substitute 1 teaspoon pure vanilla extract. If you want a thinner frosting, increase the dark rum to 3 or 4 tablespoons. If you want a thicker, richer frosting keep adding 2 tablespoons of confectioners' sugar as you beat until you reach your desired consistency.

one at a time, beating until each is incorporated. Add the vanilla and beat for 5 more seconds.

Retrieve one of the reserved portions of burnt sugar liquid. Add the flour mixture in three parts, alternating with the burnt sugar, beginning and ending with the flour mixture. Scrape down the sides and bottom of the bowl and beat again for 10 seconds. Pour the batter into the prepared pan and bake for 45 to 50 minutes, or until a small sharp knife inserted into the center of the cake comes out clean. Transfer the pan to a wire rack to cool completely. Gently loosen the sides of the cake from the pan and turn it out onto the rack.

MAKE THE CARAMEL RUM FROSTING

Put the butter, rum, confectioners' sugar, and remaining portion of burnt sugar liquid in a food processor. Pulse in short bursts until the frosting is shiny and smooth.

ASSEMBLE THE BURNT SUGAR BUNDT CAKE

Use an offset spatula to spread the frosting over the crown of the Bundt in a thick layer. Top with caramel shards, if you like (see sidebar below). Let the frosting set before serving. The cake will keep in an airtight container, at room temperature, for up to 3 days.

CARAMEL SHARD TOPPING

This caramel shard decoration is entirely optional—but it looks spectacular. Consider using it when you bring this cake to a potluck picnic in the park or a brunch.

½ cup granulated sugar

Place the sugar in a small saucepan. Add enough water—it takes approximately 1 teaspoon—to make it the texture of wet sand. Cook on high heat until the sugar turns amber. Pour the caramel onto a half-sheet pan lined with a Silpat (or other silicone nonstick) baking mat. Let cool. Break the cooled caramel into small shards and use them to decorate the frosted cake.

Ingredients

FOR THE DARK CHOCOLATE AND MALTED BUTTERCREAMS

5 large egg whites, at room temperature

1½ cups sugar

1 teaspoon pure vanilla extract

2 cups (4 sticks) unsalted butter, at room temperature

4 ounces good-quality dark chocolate (60 to 72%), melted and cooled

¼ cup malted milk powder

12 malted milk ball candies, crushed

FOR THE CHOCOLATE CAKE ROLL

1 cup all-purpose flour

¼ cup dark unsweetened cocoa powder (like Valrhona), sifted

¼ teaspoon salt

2 tablespoons instant espresso powder

12 ounces good-quality dark chocolate (60 to 72%), melted and cooled

12 large eggs, at room temperature, separated

1⅓ cups sugar

4 teaspoons pure vanilla extract

¼ teaspoon cream of tartar

6 tablespoons (¾ stick) unsalted butter, melted and cooled

Baked Note

This cake is spectacular, but it does require some thoughtful preparation. It is important to make and chill the dark chocolate and malted buttercreams before baking the cake. Also, right before you start assembling the cake, pull the buttercream out of the refrigerator so it reaches room temperature in time for filling the bûche. Finally, I suggest making the optional meringue mushrooms, the sugared cranberries, and the sugared rosemary (page **194-195**) while your filled and frosted bûche is setting up in the refrigerator.

STUMP DE NOËL

THE STUMP DE NOËL, A CHRISTMAS HOLIDAY PIÈCE DE RÉSISTANCE, IS THE BAKED INTERPRETATION OF THE INFAMOUS BÛCHE DE NOËL, UBIQUITOUS IN FRANCE. Our stump is every bit as alluring as a classic bûche, though we played with a few of the elements to make it more distinctly Baked. Our stump is an allusion to our fondness for woodland creatures, and it can be iced and finished to reflect the dinner: tongue-in-cheek, realistic, or slightly menacing. Traditionally, the bûche consists of a springy yellow sponge filled with chocolate buttercream. I made the sponge cake slightly less spongy, and the filling is chock-full of our favorite flavor, malt. I even added a little texture with crushed malt balls. Obviously, this is a slightly showy, purely holidayesque affair, but don't be afraid to make it whenever you damn well please.

YIELD: 24 SERVINGS

MAKE THE DARK CHOCOLATE AND MALTED BUTTERCREAMS

In the bowl of a standing mixer, combine the egg whites and sugar. Set the bowl over a pot of simmering water and whisk until the sugar is dissolved and the egg whites are just warm to the touch. Return the bowl to the mixer and fit it with the whisk attachment. Add the vanilla and beat the egg whites at high speed until firm and glossy, about 5 minutes. With the machine running, whisk in the butter a few tablespoons at a time. If the mixture begins to look curdled, continue to beat until it is smooth before adding more butter.

Transfer 1½ cups of the buttercream to a bowl and whisk in the melted chocolate. Cover the chocolate buttercream and refrigerate.

Dissolve the malt powder in 2 tablespoons hot water, then beat it into the buttercream remaining in the mixer. Beat in the crushed milk balls. Cover the malt buttercream and refrigerate.

MAKE THE CHOCOLATE CAKE ROLL

Preheat the oven to 350 degrees F. Butter two 17-by-12-inch rimmed baking sheets and line them with parchment paper, leaving a 1-inch overhang on all the short sides. Butter the paper and dust it with flour.

In a small bowl, whisk together the flour, cocoa powder, and salt. In another

small bowl, dissolve the espresso powder in ¼ cup hot water, then stir in the chocolate.

In the bowl of a standing mixer, whisk together the egg yolks and ⅔ cup of the sugar. Set the bowl over a pan of simmering water and whisk until the sugar is dissolved. Transfer the bowl to a mixer fitted with the whisk attachment and beat at high speed until the yolks are pale and thick, about 5 minutes. Beat in the melted chocolate mixture along with the vanilla. Transfer the mixture to a large bowl.

Thoroughly wash and dry the mixer bowl and the whisk attachment. In the clean bowl, beat the egg whites with the cream of tartar on medium-high speed until soft peaks form. Gradually add the remaining ⅔ cup sugar and continue beating at high speed until the whites are glossy, about 2 minutes longer. Whisk a quarter of the egg whites into the cake batter, then fold in the remaining whites until no streaks remain.

In a small bowl, whisk the melted butter with ½ cup of the batter; fold this mixture into the batter. In two batches, sift the cocoa powder mixture over the batter and gently fold it in. Divide the batter between the prepared pans and use an offset spatula to spread it evenly.

Bake the cakes for about 18 minutes, until they feel springy and slightly dry; shift the pans from top to bottom and front to back halfway through the baking time. Transfer the pans to wire racks and cool completely. Run the tip of a knife around the edges, cover the cake surface with parchment paper and a baking sheet, and turn it out of the pan; peel off the parchment liner.

TO ASSEMBLE THE CAKE

Spread the malt buttercream over the cakes. Using a ruler, cut each cake precisely in half lengthwise, cutting through the parchment lining them; you should have four 6 by 17-inch strips of cake. Roll one strip into a tight coil, removing the paper as you roll. Roll the three remaining cake strips around the coil in the same way to form a very wide, short jelly roll. Set the cake on a large plate, spiraled end up. Frost the outside of the cake with the chocolate buttercream. Refrigerate the cake until set, at least 8 hours. If desired, decorate it with the meringue mushrooms, cranberries, and rosemary sprigs, and serve, cutting the cake into wedges or horizontal slices. (We like to cut the stump lengthwise for the full effect. It is thin, but large.)

QUICK SKILLET SNACK CAKE

A GOOD, SOLID, EASY-TO-PUT-TOGETHER, AND EASY-TO-BAKE SNACKIN' CAKE SHOULD BE PART OF EVERY HOME BAKER'S REPERTOIRE, AND THIS IS OUR GO-TO SOLUTION. It's a springy chocolate cake with a slathering of fudgy frosting and my favorite part: It's baked in a skillet, which gives the sides a fun crunch. This is the cake I make when I have a hankering for something less celebratory and more quick and dirty—the kind of cake I can throw together for an impromptu afternoon gathering. If I am toting the cake to a destination, I put the whole thing back in the skillet for ease in carrying.

YIELD: ONE 10-INCH SKILLET CAKE

MAKE THE CHOCOLATE CAKE

Preheat the oven to 350 degrees F.

Grease a 10-inch, cast-iron skillet or ovenproof stainless-steel skillet with butter. (The heavy, dark-colored cast-iron skillet will make the sides of the cake more crispy than a stainless steel one.) Line the pan with parchment paper and butter the parchment. Dust the parchment with flour and knock out the excess.

In a small, heatproof bowl, whisk together the cocoa powder, chocolate, and espresso powder. Add ¾ cup very hot water, wait 1 minute, and then whisk the mixture until it is melted and smooth. Set aside to cool.

In another small bowl, whisk together the flour, baking soda, and salt.

In the bowl of a standing mixer fitted with the paddle attachment, beat the butter and shortening together on medium speed until creamy, 2 to 3 minutes. Add the sugars and vanilla and beat until fluffy, about 3 minutes. Scrape down the bowl, add the eggs one at a time, and beat until just combined. Turn the mixer to its lowest setting, and in a slow, steady stream, add the reserved chocolate mixture. Scrape down the bowl again, then turn the mixer to low. Add the flour mixture in three parts, alternating with the buttermilk, begin-

½ cup unsweetened dark cocoa powder (like Valrhona)

2 ounces good-quality dark chocolate (60 to 72%), coarsely chopped

1 teaspoon instant espresso powder

1½ cups all-purpose flour

1 teaspoon baking soda

1 teaspoon salt

½ cup (1 stick) unsalted butter, cut into 1-inch cubes, at room temperature

2 tablespoons vegetable shortening, at room temperature

1 cup firmly packed dark brown sugar

¼ cup granulated sugar

1 teaspoon pure vanilla extract

3 large eggs

¼ cup plus 2 tablespoons buttermilk, shaken vigorously

FOR THE CHOCOLATE FROSTING

½ cup (1 stick) unsalted butter, softened

1 cup confectioners' sugar, sifted

1 tablespoon pure vanilla extract

3 ounces good-quality dark chocolate (60 to 72%), melted and cooled

Baked Note

I often get asked about the necessity of using shortening in this recipe. Do you have to do it? Not really. Can you replace it with butter? Yes, I suppose. Just note that shortening gives the cake a really great springy texture, and shortening is not necessarily the devil it is made out to be. Crisco, the classic vegetable shortening, makes a trans-fat-free version, and Spectrum Naturals makes an organic trans-fat-free version.

ning and ending with the flour mixture. Scrape down the bowl, then mix for a few more seconds and pour the batter into the prepared skillet. Smooth the surface with a spatula.

Bake for 40 to 45 minutes, rotating the skillet halfway through the baking time, until a toothpick inserted in the center of the cake comes out clean. Transfer the pan to a wire rack to cool for about 15 minutes. Run a paring knife around the sides of the pan and flip the cake out onto a cooling rack. Turn the cake right side up and let it sit on the rack until completely cool.

MAKE THE CHOCOLATE FROSTING

In the bowl of a standing mixer fitted with the paddle attachment, beat the butter on high speed until creamy, about 2 minutes. Add the confectioners' sugar all at once and beat until completely blended, about 2 minutes. Add the vanilla and beat for 15 seconds. Scrape down the bowl and add the melted, cooled chocolate. Beat until smooth, continuing to scrape down the sides of the bowl as needed until the frosting is uniform in color.

Transfer the skillet cake to a cake board or serving platter. Use an offset spatula to spread the frosting evenly across the top. Serve it immediately or refrigerate it, if necessary. Bring it back to room temperature before serving.

LADY PRALINE CHIFFON CAKE

I FEEL LIKE I WAS BORN AT THE TAIL END OF THE CHIFFON CRAZE. It is as if the chiffon, a slightly denser cousin of angel food cake, was in vogue for a lifetime, then slowly drifted into irrelevance, like coq au vin. I remember chiffon cakes as regal affairs baked by regal ladies of a certain age, the kind of ladies who wore a large brooch pinned to their expensive jacket.

The chiffon cake was invented in California (the aptly named Harry Baker is credited with being its creator), but our Lady Praline Chiffon is dedicated to all stately Southern ladies and to the pecan.

YIELD: ONE 10-INCH TUBE CAKE

Preheat the oven to 325 degrees F. In a medium bowl, use your hands to rub the dark brown sugar into the granulated sugar until all lumps are gone and the sugars are combined. In a large bowl, sift the flour, baking powder, and salt together. Whisk the sugar mixture into the flour mixture.

In another bowl, whisk together the egg yolks, the egg, and liqueur until smooth. Stir in the oil and ½ cup water until combined. Make a well in the center of the dry ingredients and pour the wet mixture into it. Use a rubber spatula to fold the wet ingredients into the dry ingredients, add the orange zest, and fold until just combined. Do not overmix.

In a clean bowl, whisk the egg whites, cream of tartar, and orange zest until stiff peaks form. Do not overbeat. Gently fold the egg whites into the batter and pour it into an ungreased 10-inch tube pan, with a removable bottom.

Bake the cake for 50 to 60 minutes, rotating the pan halfway through the baking time, until a toothpick inserted in the center comes out clean. Invert the pan over a wire rack to cool completely, about 2 hours. (If the cake has risen above the top of the pan, invert it onto the neck of a bottle to hold it aloft.) To release the cake, run an offset metal spatula along the inner and outer edges of the pan. Sprinkle the wire rack with a little confectioners' sugar so the cake will not stick, and place the cake on the rack. Sprinkle slices with confectioners' sugar before serving.

Ingredients

¼ cup firmly packed dark brown sugar

½ cup plus 2 tablespoons granulated sugar

1¼ cups cake flour

2 teaspoons baking powder

½ teaspoon salt

5 egg yolks plus 1 egg

1 tablespoon pecan liqueur (if you can find it—otherwise, use an almond liqueur like Amaretto, or pure almond extract)

¾ cup vegetable oil

5 egg whites

¼ teaspoon cream of tartar

zest of 1 small to medium orange

Baked Note

You are either a chiffon person or not. Chiffon, like angel food cake, is butter-free, and the cake has a springy crumb that people tend either to adore or abhor. For those who like it, nothing is better for a summer soiree than a light chiffon.

CHOCOLATE COFFEE CAKE
WITH DARK CHOCOLATE GANACHE

THE CHOCOLATE COFFEE CAKE IS PURE EGO. It is a basic Baked creation that does not readily fit into any regional or historical category. It is a perennial customer favorite, and the recipe is requested often enough to demand inclusion in this book. The chocolate cake is dark, moist, and inviting, while the coffee buttercream filling and frosting is a bit adult without leaving an extreme coffee aftertaste. The entire three-layer affair is dressed in a thick, drippy, sexy chocolate ganache and studded with chocolate-covered espresso beans. It looks like fall and tastes like heaven. If you are coffee-averse, I promise you will enjoy this cake nonetheless. The coffee flavor is subtle and smooth, but necessary, in that it contrasts perfectly with the dark chocolate.

YIELD: ONE 8-INCH, 3-LAYER CAKE

MAKE THE CLASSIC CHOCOLATE CAKE

Preheat the oven to 325 degrees F. Butter three 8-inch round cake pans, line them with parchment paper, and butter the parchment. Dust the parchment with flour and knock out the excess flour.

In a medium bowl, mix the cocoa powder and sour cream with 1¼ cups hot water and set aside to cool.

In a large bowl, sift the flour, baking soda, baking powder, and salt together and set aside.

Using a standing mixer fitted with the paddle attachment, beat the butter and shortening together on medium speed until light and fluffy, about 5 minutes—the mixture will appear to string or ribbon throughout the bowl. Add the sugars and beat on medium speed until light and fluffy, about 5 more minutes. Add the eggs, one at a time, mixing about 10 to 15 seconds after each addition until the egg is incorporated into the mixture. Then turn the mixer to low, add the vanilla, and beat until incorporated. Scrape down the sides of the bowl and mix again for 30 seconds.

Beginning with the dry ingredients, add the dry mixture and the cocoa mixture to the mixer bowl in three alternating parts, ending with dry.

Divide the batter among the prepared pans. Use an offset spatula to level the batter. Bake the cakes for 35 to 40 minutes, rotating the pans halfway through the baking time, until a toothpick inserted in the center comes out clean. Transfer the pans to a wire rack and cool for 30 to 45 minutes. Turn the cakes out onto the rack and let them cool completely. Remove the parchment.

MAKE THE COFFEE BUTTERCREAM

In a medium, heavy-bottomed saucepan, whisk the sugar and flour together. Add the milk and cream and cook over medium heat, whisking occasionally, until the mixture comes to a boil and has thickened, about 10 to 15 minutes.

Transfer the mixture to the bowl of a standing mixer fitted with the paddle attachment. Beat on high speed until cool (this takes about 7 to 9 minutes of mixing; however, you can speed up the process by pressing bags of frozen berries or frozen corn around the sides and bottom of the mixing bowl). Reduce the speed to low and add the butter; mix until thoroughly incorporated. Increase the speed to medium-high and beat until the frosting is light and fluffy, about another 1 to 2 minutes.

Add the vanilla and coffee extracts and continue mixing until combined. If the frosting is too soft, put the bowl in the refrigerator to chill slightly, then beat again until it is the proper consistency. If the frosting is too firm, set the bowl over a pot of simmering water and beat with a wooden spoon until it is the proper consistency.

TO ASSEMBLE THE CAKE

Place one cake layer on a serving platter. Trim the top to create a flat surface, and evenly spread about 1¼ cups frosting on top. Add the next layer, trim and frost it, then add the third layer. Spread a very thin layer of frosting over the sides and top of the cake and put it in the refrigerator for about 15 minutes to firm up. (This is known as crumb coating and will help to keep loose cake crumbs under control when you frost the outside of the cake.) Spread the sides and top of the cake with the remaining frosting. Refrigerate it for 15 minutes to it firm up.

MAKE THE CHOCOLATE GLAZE

Place the chocolate, butter, and corn syrup in the top of a double boiler. Using a rubber spatula, stir the mixture until the chocolate and butter are completely melted and smooth.

Remove the pan from the heat and stir the glaze to release excess heat. Drizzle glaze over the cake. Refrigerate the cake for about 15 minutes to set the glaze before serving.

GLAZE THE CAKE

Line a rimmed baking sheet with parchment paper. Place your cake on a wire rack over the baking sheet. Slowly pour about ¾ cup of the glaze over the cake. Use a small offset spatula to smooth it out to the edges. Place the cake in the refrigerator for 5 minutes to set the glaze. Remove from the refrigerator and slowly pour the rest of the glaze over the cake. It should run down the edges in thick streams. You should be able to control the size and length of the streams by the pour. Feel free to experiment, and have no fear in playing around. This is the fun part, and there is no right or wrong way. Garnish with chocolate-covered espresso beans. Chill the entire cake for approximately 20 minutes, or until glaze is set, then transfer to cake plate. Serve at room temperature.

The cake can be stored, covered in a cake dome or cake saver, at room temperature for up to 3 days.

FOR THE TOMATO SOUP CUPCAKES

2 (10¾-ounce) cans condensed tomato soup, preferably low-sodium

1 teaspoon baking soda

3½ cups all-purpose flour

1½ teaspoons cinnamon

½ teaspoon freshly grated nutmeg

½ teaspoon ground allspice

¼ teaspoon salt

1 teaspoon baking powder

¾ cup (1½ sticks) unsalted butter, at room temperature

1 cup granulated sugar

1 cup firmly packed light brown sugar

4 large eggs

FOR THE MASCARPONE FROSTING

¾ cup (1½ sticks) unsalted butter, softened

12 ounces mascarpone cheese, softened

4 cups confectioners' sugar, sifted

1 teaspoon pure vanilla extract

Baked Note

Feeling really adventurous? In the mood for something even a little strange? Try making these cupcakes a play on sweet/savory. Omit the cinnamon, nutmeg, and allspice; replace them with 1 teaspoon freshly ground pepper and increase the salt to ½ teaspoon.

TOMATO SOUP CUPCAKES
WITH MASCARPONE FROSTING

THE TOMATO SOUP CUPCAKE DESERVES SOME EXPLANATION. Though the unusual main ingredient adds a hint of kitsch to the recipe, it makes for a moist and easy-to-put-together cupcake. Additionally, it brings an interesting flavor to the over-saturated cupcake market (don't worry—the tomato taste is not prominent). If you're tired of the same vanilla-frosted chocolate cake, this recipe merits your attention. Tomato soup cake does not dominate a certain region, though it seems to have touched a nerve with a great many Midwestern grandmothers (according to our nonscientific study). This recipe is based on one that originally served as the foundation for a spice cake. We tinkered with it to tone down the spice so that the tang provided by the tomato soup is not completely overwhelmed. Feeling adventurous? Try this recipe.

YIELD: **24** CUPCAKES

MAKE THE TOMATO SOUP CUPCAKES

Preheat the oven to 325 degrees F. Line two 12-cup cupcake pans with paper liners.

In a large bowl, sprinkle the baking soda over the top of the tomato soup and stir well. Set aside.

In a medium bowl, sift together the flour, cinnamon, nutmeg, allspice, salt, and baking powder.

In the bowl of a standing mixer fitted with the paddle attachment, beat the butter and both sugars together on medium speed until fluffy, 3 to 4 minutes. Add the eggs, one at a time, and beat until just combined. Scrape down the sides and bottom of the bowl and beat for a few seconds. Turn the mixer to low. Add the flour mixture in three parts, alternating with the tomato soup, beginning and ending with the flour mixture. Scrape down the bowl again, and mix on low speed for a few more seconds.

Fill the prepared cupcake pan about three-quarters full. Bake the cupakes for 25 to 28 minutes, or until a toothpick inserted in the center of a cupcake comes out clean.

Allow the cupcakes to cool for 30 minutes in the pan, then turn them out onto wire racks to cool completely.

MAKE THE MASCARPONE FROSTING

In the bowl of a standing mixer fitted with the paddle attachment, beat the softened butter until it is completely smooth. Add the mascarpone and beat until combined.

Add the sugar and vanilla and beat until smooth. Be careful not to overbeat; this will cause the frosting to lose structure. (At this point, if you want to, you can tightly cover the frosting and refrigerate it overnight. Let it soften at room temperature before using.)

TO ASSEMBLE THE CUPCAKES

If you have a pastry bag, simply fit it with the largest tip, fill the bag with frosting, and pipe enough over each cake to cover the cupcake with a big mound. If you do not have a pastry bag, use an ice cream scoop with a release mechanism to scoop the frosting and dispense it onto the top of the cupcake. You can also use an offset spatula to frost the cupcakes.

Refrigerate any leftover cupcakes in an airtight container for up to 3 days. Bring the cupcakes to room temperature before serving.

FOR THE CHOCOLATE COOKIE CRUST

16 ounces chocolate sandwich cookies such as Oreos (35 to 40 cookes), crushed

5 tablespoons unsalted butter, melted

FOR THE FLOURLESS CHOCOLATE CAKE

4 tablespoons (½ stick) unsalted butter

6 ounces good-quality dark chocolate (60 to 70%), chopped

2 tablespoons plus 1 teaspoon instant espresso powder

¼ cup strong coffee, at room temperature

¼ teaspoon salt

1 tablespoon pure vanilla extract

6 large eggs, separated, at room temperature

1 cup sugar

FOR THE CHOCOLATE PUDDING

¾ cup sugar

½ cup dark unsweetened cocoa powder (like Valrhona)

¼ cup cornstarch

¼ teaspoon salt

4 large egg yolks

2½ cups whole milk

3 tablespoons unsalted butter

2 teaspoons pure vanilla extract

3 ounces good-quality dark chocolate (60 to 70%)

ASSEMBLY

Simple Whipped Cream (page 159)

Baked Note

This is an easy, though many-stepped, recipe. Don't fear, just break up the parts over the course of two days. Make the cookie crust and cake on day one, and make the pudding on the day you're going to serve the dessert. Keep in mind that the cake requires 3 hours to set before it can be cut. The whipped cream topping can be made 15 minutes before serving.

MISSISSIPPI MUD PIE (B),
AKA MUDDY MISSISSIPPI CAKE

THOUGH MISSISSIPPI MUD PIE WAS A STAPLE OF SOUTHERN MENUS DURING MY COLLEGIATE YOUTH, THERE IS NO REAL INDICATION THAT THIS DESSERT WAS CREATED IN MISSISSIPPI (OR EVEN THE SOUTH). To further complicate matters, it seems that Mississippi mud pie (or cake) varies widely in interpretation and means many things to many people. If I had to identify the characteristics of a typical Mississippi mud, I'd say it is a very dense, very sweet chocolate cake. Fudgy comes to mind. It is also probably covered or made with marshmallows and topped with pecans and chocolate sauce. The usual Mississippi mud is far too sweet and strangely dense for my taste buds these days, so I created a dreamier, more elegant version. I bake a flourless chocolate cake inside a cookie crust and top it with a layer of silky chocolate pudding and whipped cream. It is, by far, the Baked staff favorite.

YIELD: ONE 9-INCH ROUND CAKE

MAKE THE CHOCOLATE COOKIE CRUST

Preheat the oven to 300 degrees F. Lightly spray a 9-inch springform pan with nonstick cooking spray. Line the pan with parchment paper and lightly spray the parchment and sides of the pan.

In a food processor, grind the cookies to a very fine crumb. You should have about 3½ cups. Put the crumbs in a small bowl. Pour the melted butter over them and mix with a rubber spatula until well combined.

Turn the crumb mixture into the prepared pan and press it into the bottom and up the sides, leaving about ½ inch between the top of the crust and the top of the pan. Use the back of a large spoon to get an even layer of crust. Place the pan in the freezer and let the crust set for about 10 minutes.

Bake the crust in the oven until it is dry to the touch, about 10 minutes. Transfer the pan to a wire rack and let cool.

MAKE THE FLOURLESS CHOCOLATE CAKE

Increase the oven temperature to 350 degrees F.

Using a double boiler or microwave (page 16), melt the butter and chocolate together. Set aside to cool.

In a small bowl, whisk together the espresso powder, coffee, salt, and vanilla. Set aside.

In the bowl of a standing mixer fitted with the whisk attachment, beat the egg yolks with ½ cup of the sugar until the mixture is light and has almost doubled in volume, about 5 minutes. Add the chocolate mixture and beat until just combined. Scrape down the sides and bottom of the bowl and mix on low speed for 5 seconds. Add the coffee mixture and beat until just combined. Scrape down the sides and bottom of the bowl and mix on low for 5 seconds.

In a clean bowl fitted with the whisk attachment (or you can elect to do this step by hand if you are feeling strong), beat the egg whites until foamy. Gradually increase the speed to high and add the remaining ½ cup sugar, beating until soft peaks form.

Scoop 1 cup of the egg whites into the chocolate mixture. Use a rubber spatula to gently fold in the egg whites. After about 30 seconds of folding, add the remaining egg whites and continue folding until they are almost completely combined. Do not rush the folding process, work gently, and take care not to overmix. Pour the batter onto the cooled cookie crust and bake for 38 to 42 minutes, until the cake is set but still jiggles slightly. It might not appear to be completely cooked. Transfer it to a wire rack and cool completely. (As it cools, the cake will deflate in the center and look sunken. Do not despair, this is just the way it settles.) Tightly wrap and refrigerate the cake for at least three hours or overnight.

MAKE THE CHOCOLATE PUDDING

In a medium saucepan, whisk together the sugar, cocoa powder, cornstarch, and salt. Add the egg yolks and whisk until combined. The mixture will look like a thick paste. Slowly pour in the milk, whisking constantly.

In a saucepan over medium heat, bring the mixture to a boil, whisking constantly to prevent it from burning on the bottom of the pan. Boil for 30 seconds, then transfer it to a medium bowl. Add the butter, vanilla, and chocolate and whisk until combined. Continue to whisk for a few more minutes to cool the mixture slightly. Let the pudding stand for 15 minutes at room temperature. Press a piece of plastic wrap directly onto the surface of the pudding to prevent a skin from forming, and chill it for at least 3 hours.

TO ASSEMBLE THE MISSISSIPPI MUD PIE

Stir the pudding to loosen it, then pour it on top of the cake, making sure to stay inside the cookie-crust border. Use an offset spatula to spread the pudding into an even layer. Return the cake to the refrigerator for at least 30 minutes while you prepare the whipped cream topping. Spread whipped cream across the pudding layer, all the way out to the sides, unmold the cake, and serve it immediately.

The cake can be kept, covered, in the refrigerator for up to 2 days.

SIMPLE WHIPPED CREAM

1¼ cups heavy cream
2 tablespoons granulated sugar

Pour the cream into a chilled metal bowl and beat with a chilled whisk for about 1 minute or until soft peaks form. Sprinkle the sugar on the cream and continue whisking vigorously until stiff peaks form.

Yield: about 2 cups whipped cream

Ingredients

Ingredients

FOR THE MAPLE CUPCAKES

3 cups all-purpose flour

3 teaspoons baking powder

1 teaspoon salt

½ cup (1 stick) butter, slightly softened, cut into chunks

2 tablespoons vegetable shortening, at room temperature

2 cups pure maple syrup (I use grade B to bake with but any grade will suffice)

3 egg yolks

1 large egg

1¼ cups whole milk

1 cup walnuts, toasted and coarsely chopped

FOR THE CREAM CHEESE MAPLE FROSTING

¾ cup (1½ sticks) unsalted butter, softened

12 ounces cream cheese, softened

4 cups confectioners' sugar, sifted

2 tablespoons maple syrup

ASSEMBLY

Whole toasted walnuts (optional)

Baked Note

Do not, I repeat, do not use imitation maple syrup in this recipe. Actually, avoid imitation maple syrup at all times. It is usually composed of corn syrup and food coloring and, sadly, contains very little, if any, real maple syrup. In short, it's hard to think of a more disingenuous grocery store product.

MAPLE CUPCAKES
WITH MAPLE CREAM CHEESE FROSTING

THOUGH IT MAY BE A CLICHÉ IN THIS COUNTRY, VERMONT IS VIRTUALLY SYNONYMOUS WITH MAPLE SYRUP. Maple festivals figure heavily into the Vermont calendar, and all manner of maple merchandise (aprons, magnets, candies, cookbooks . . .) is available for purchase in the retail shops that line many of Vermont's historic towns. Real maple syrup deserves its reputation. It gives these cupcakes a great robust flavor, moist crumb, and golden brown color, while the cream cheese frosting with a touch of maple syrup provides the perfect accompaniment. The cupcakes are truly autumnal, but I encourage you to make them during any season you please.

YIELD: 24 CUPCAKES

MAKE THE MAPLE CUPCAKES

Preheat the oven to 325 degrees F. Line two 12-cup cupcake pans with paper liners.

In a medium bowl, sift together the flour, baking powder, and salt.

In the bowl of a standing mixer fitted with the paddle attachment, beat the butter and shortening until ribbonlike. Turn the mixer to low and stream in the maple syrup. Increase the speed to medium-high and beat until the mixture is nearly uniform in color, about 3 minutes.

Add the egg yolks and egg, one at a time, and beat until just incorporated. Scrape down the sides and bottom of the bowl. Add half of the flour mixture and mix on low speed until incorporated. Stream in the milk. Stop the mixer, add the rest of the flour, then turn the mixer on until just combined. Scrape down the sides and bottom of the bowl and fold in the walnuts.

Fill the prepared cupcake pan about three-quarters full. Bake the cupcakes for 20 to 25 minutes, rotating the pans halfway through the baking time, until a toothpick inserted in the center of a cupcake comes out clean. Note: These cupcakes take longer to bake than traditional cupcakes due to the maple syrup.

Allow the cupcakes to cool for 15 minutes in the cupcake pan, then turn them out onto wire racks to cool completely.

MAKE THE CREAM CHEESE MAPLE FROSTING

In the bowl of a standing mixer fitted with the paddle attachment, beat the softened butter until it is completely smooth. Add the cream cheese and beat until combined.

Add the sugar and the maple syrup and beat until smooth. Be careful not to overbeat the frosting or it will lose structure. (At this point, if you want to, you can tightly cover the frosting and refrigerate it for a day. Let it soften at room temperature before using.)

ASSEMBLE THE CUPCAKES

There are many ways to frost a cupcake. If you have a pastry bag, simply fit with the largest tip, fill the bag with frosting, and pipe enough to cover the cupcake in a big mound. If you do not have a pastry bag, use an ice cream scoop with a release mechanism to scoop the frosting and dispense it onto the top of the cupcake. You can also use an offset spatula to frost the cupcakes. Top with whole toasted walnuts.

Refrigerate any leftover cupcakes in an airtight container for up to 3 days. Bring cupcakes to room temperature before serving.

SUNDAY NIGHT CAKE

THE WONDERFUL SUNDAY NIGHT CAKE, AS ITS NAME IMPLIES, IS A GREAT WAY TO END A WEEKEND. It is a no-frills affair—no layers to fill, no curds to set, no egg whites to whip. It is just an exceedingly pleasing, simple, and delicious gently spiced sour cream cake with easy chocolate frosting. The theme behind Sunday Night Cake is ease and comfort. Therefore, if your guests are seeking something more complicated, like a six-layer cake or a roulade, they should be directed elsewhere or asked to return on a different night (say, Friday). Our pastry chef, Eric Wolitzky, stumbled upon this cake while entering his Edna Lewis phase. Although he loves the original recipe and Edna Lewis, the grande dame of Southern cooking, his version is decidedly more Baked. Eric toyed with the crumb to make it springier, and he covered the cake in a puddinglike chocolate frosting. Even so, it is still faithful in spirit to the beloved original.

YIELD: ONE 9-INCH SQUARE CAKE

MAKE THE CAKE

Preheat the oven to 350 degrees F. Line a 9-inch square cake pan with parchment paper and butter the sides and bottom of the parchment paper.

In a large bowl, sift together the flour, baking powder, salt, and cinnamon. Set aside.

In the bowl of a standing mixer fitted with the paddle attachment, beat the butter and both sugars on medium speed until light and fluffy, about 2 minutes. Add the eggs, one at a time, and beat until just incorporated. Scrape down the sides and bottom of the bowl and beat for a few seconds. Turn the mixer to low. Add the flour mixture in three parts, alternating with the sour cream, beginning and ending with the flour mixture. Scrape down the bowl and beat for a few more seconds.

Pour the batter into the prepared pan and bake for 35 to 40 minutes, or until a toothpick inserted in the center comes out clean. Set the pan on a wire rack to cool for at least 20 minutes, loosen the sides of the cake from the pan then turn the cake out onto the rack. Remove the parchment and flip the cake right side up. Let the cake completely cool.

Ingredients

FOR THE CAKE

1¾ cups cake flour

2 teaspoons baking powder

1 teaspoon salt

½ teaspoon cinnamon

10 tablespoons (1¼ sticks) unsalted butter, at room temperature, cut into ½-inch pieces

¾ cup granulated sugar

½ cup firmly packed light brown sugar

3 large eggs

1 cup sour cream

FOR THE CHOCOLATE FROSTING

¾ cup plus 2 tablespoons granulated sugar

3½ tablespoons cornstarch

2 tablespoons dark unsweetened cocoa powder (like Valrhona)

3 ounces good-quality unsweetened chocolate, coarsely chopped

6 tablespoons (¾ stick) unsalted butter, cut into ½-inch pieces, at room temperature

Baked Note

If you want your Sunday Night Cake to be truly hassle free, you can opt out of making the frosting (although we really, really like the frosting) and sprinkle the top of the cake with some confectioners' sugar instead.

MAKE THE CHOCOLATE FROSTING

In a medium saucepan, whisk together the sugar, cornstarch, and cocoa powder. Add the chopped chocolate. Pour 1 cup boiling water into the pan, wait 30 seconds, then whisk until the mixture is combined and the chocolate is melted.

Turn the heat to medium-high and whisk continuously for about 5 minutes, or until the mixture begins to thicken. (Once pudding begins to thicken, it will come together very quickly.)

Remove the pan from the heat and pour the mixture into the bowl of a standing mixer fitted with the paddle attachment. Beat on high until the steam escapes and the mixture is room temperature. Add the butter and mix for an additional 2 to 3 minutes, until the frosting is light and puddinglike. If you prefer a fluffier, more spreadable frosting, continue to mix for a few minutes longer.

Frost the top of the cake, allowing a little of the frosting to drip down the edges. Chill for 5 minutes to set the frosting. Serve immediately.

The cake can be stored, tightly covered, in the refrigerator for up to 3 days. Bring it back to room temperature before serving.

AUNT SASSY CAKE

A DESSERT THAT LINGERS IN MY SUBCONSCIOUS ON A NEAR-CONSTANT BASIS IS BAKED'S AUNT SASSY CAKE. I have an unhealthy attachment to this cake. The light cake layers are studded with a heap of crushed pistachios, and the entire thing is filled and frosted with whipped honey vanilla buttercream. It is a dream cake, the kind you will make once every now and then but remember often. It is not a one-bowl, whip-it-up-in-an-hour cake, and it is limited to events where nut allergies are not a problem. Oh, about the name: It shall forever remain cloaked in secrecy. Suffice it to say that neither of us actually has an Aunt Sassy.

YIELD: ONE 8-INCH, 3-LAYER CAKE

MAKE THE CAKE

Preheat the oven to 325 degrees F. Butter three 8-inch round cake pans, line the bottoms with parchment paper, and butter the parchment. Dust the parchment with flour and knock out the excess flour.

In the bowl of a food processor, pulse the pistachios until they are coarsely chopped. Transfer about 2 tablespoons' worth of the coarse pistachios to a large bowl. Continue to process the rest of the pistachios until they are almost powdery—but not a superfine dust. Stir the pistachio powder into the reserved coarse pistachios. Sift the flours, baking powder, baking soda, and salt together over the large bowl containing the pistachio mix. Stir to combine.

In the bowl of a standing mixer fitted with the paddle attachment, beat the butter and shortening on medium speed until creamy, 3 to 4 minutes. Add the sugar and vanilla and beat until fluffy, about 3 minutes. Scrape down the bowl, add the whole egg, and beat until just combined. Turn the mixer to low.

In a measuring cup, make 1½ cups ice water. Add the flour mixture to the mixer in three parts, alternating with the ice water, beginning and ending with the flour mixture. For each addition, turn the mixer to low to add ingredients, then up to medum speed for a few seconds until incorporated. Scrape down the bowl, then mix on low speed for a few more seconds.

In a medium bowl, whisk the egg whites and cream of tartar until soft peaks form (You can do this by hand. Don't be intimidated, it should only take 2 to 3 minutes). Do not overbeat. Gently fold the egg whites into the batter.

Ingredients

CAKE

1 cup shelled pistachios

2½ cups cake flour

¾ cup all-purpose flour

1 tablespoon baking powder

1 teaspoon baking soda

¾ teaspoon salt

½ cup (1 stick) unsalted butter, softened

½ cup vegetable shortening

1¾ cups sugar

1 tablespoon pure vanilla extract

1 large egg

3 large egg whites, at room temperature

¼ teaspoon cream of tartar

HONEY VANILLA BUTTERCREAM

1½ cups sugar

⅓ cup all-purpose flour

1½ cups whole milk

⅓ cup heavy cream

1½ cups (3 sticks) unsalted butter, soft but cool, cut into small pieces

1 teaspoon pure vanilla extract

3 tablespoons honey

ASSEMBLY

⅓ cup crushed shelled pistachios

Baked Note

Unfortunately and fortunately, I have never been able to control myself around pistachios. I suppose, left unchecked, I could devour my weight in pistachios in a few hours. That said, I have a few friends who seem unaware that nuts can go stale rather quickly (and this has created some slightly uncomfortable after-dinner moments). Left at room temperature, pistachios should be eaten within a few days to a week at the latest from purchase—check the package for specific freshness information. They can be stored in an airtight container in the refrigerator for up to 2 months.

Divide the batter among the prepared pans and smooth the tops. Bake for 40 to 45 minutes, rotating the pans halfway through the baking time, until a toothpick inserted in the center of the cake comes out clean. Transfer the pans to a wire rack and let cool for 20 minutes. Turn the cakes out onto the rack and let cool completely. Remove the parchment paper.

MAKE THE HONEY VANILLA BUTTERCREAM

In a medium, heavy-bottomed saucepan, whisk the sugar and flour together. Add the milk and cream and cook over medium heat, whisking occasionally, until the mixture comes to a boil and has thickened, about 10 to 15 minutes.

Transfer the mixture to the bowl of a standing mixer fitted with the paddle attachment. Beat on high speed until cool (this takes at least 7 to 9 minutes of mixing; you can speed up the process by pressing bags of frozen berries or frozen corn against the sides and bottom of the mixing bowl). Reduce the speed to low and add the butter; mix until thoroughly incorporated. Increase the speed to medium-high and beat until the frosting is light and fluffy, 1 to 2 minutes.

Add the vanilla and honey and continue mixing until combined. If the frosting is too soft, put the bowl in the refrigerator to chill slightly, then beat again until it is the proper consistency. If the frosting is too firm, set the bowl over a pot of simmering water and beat with a wooden spoon until it is the proper consistency.

ASSEMBLE THE CAKE

Place one cake layer on a serving platter. Trim the top to create a flat surface, and evenly spread about 1¼ cups frosting on top. Add the next layer, trim and frost it, then add the third layer. Spread a very thin layer of frosting over the sides and top of the cake and put it in the refrigerator for about 15 minutes to firm up. (This is known as crumb coating and will help to keep loose cake crumbs under control when you frost the outside of the cake.) Spread the sides and top of the cake with the remaining frosting. Garnish the cake with crushed pistachios and refrigerate it for 15 minutes to it firm up before serving.

This cake will keep beautifully in a cake saver at room temperature for up to 3 days, if the weather is cool and humidity free. Otherwise, put it in a cake saver and refrigerate it for up to 3 days. Let the cake sit at room temperature for at least 2 hours before serving.

5

CONFECTIONS AND PASTRY

My family had a candy bowl, not a dish. It was nothing extraordinary, just a nondescript and nicked soup bowl filled with candy. At various times, the bowl held Jolly Ranchers, lollipops, M&Ms, individually wrapped caramels, and Hershey's Kisses (by far the most common bowl filler). During the holidays, the ordinary candy bowl was whisked away and replaced with a fanciful red and green holiday dish, but it reappeared on December 26. I loved that candy bowl.

As expected, on a few occasions, I overindulged. I still do. I am a recovering candy addict, and I no longer leave myself open to temptation by setting out extraneous candy bowls, dishes, or multipack candy bar minis. Now, when I have a hankering for candy, I make it instead. The process, like baking, is soothing; plus, lately I have a thing for candy thermometers and chemistry.

At the moment, I am an amateur candy maker with great aspirations. I am happy to report that while I was researching this book, many people submitted recipes that showed a dizzying grasp of the science involved. Like the handwritten, almost philosophical digression on spun sugar. No, that didn't make this book. Quite simply, those recipe suggestions were more ambitious than I had predicted. I intend to attempt a spun sugar cage shortly, but I need to develop my candy-making skills further. In the meantime,

I've included a few regional favorites. Buckeyes (see page 172) are known for both their kid-friendly approach and addictive combo of peanut butter, chocolate, and graham, while the Marshmallow Chocolate Cups (see page 178) are a riff on an old-time candy. Making those dark-chocolate cups filled with marshmallow gave me a feeling of accomplishment that I'd imagine is usually reserved for worldly chocolatiers.

This is also the chapter where I stuffed in some of the more interesting—er, stuff that defies a label—items. I can honestly say that Strawberry Jell-O Salad (see page 183), which is not really a salad, is one of the strangest but most popular items I made. My taste testers still ask when I might be making that "Jell-O strawberry pretzel thing" again. I also had to find a place for the lovely banana fritters, which are easy and should be made more often. Finally, I recommend everyone take a crack at the Caramel Popcorn (see page 189). It is sinful. And it makes the most amazing gift.

Ingredients

¼ cup cream cheese, softened

1½ cups peanut butter

1 cup graham cracker crumbs (about 14 graham crackers)

3 cups confectioners' sugar

10 tablespoons (1¼ sticks) unsalted butter, melted and cooled

12 ounces good-quality dark chocolate (60 to 72%), coarsely chopped

Baked Note:

This recipe is fun for large parties and big gatherings. Just pass them around like hors d'oeuvres—they make perfect finger food. Also, feel free to substitute chunky peanut butter for smooth peanut butter; however, be aware that all-natural versions do not work as well.

BUCKEYES

I GREW UP WITH THIS DEEPLY REGIONAL CLASSIC CANDY. Fear not, there is no gauzy colored memory attached, it was just the one candy my mom (not exactly a friend of the kitchen) would make repeatedly because it was both quick and easy. And truly tasty. The buckeye is perhaps best known to those in Ohio and the surrounding states. Judging by the reactions of a sampling of friends, it is almost completely unknown on the coasts. I present you with a less sweet version than the one Mom used to make (less sweet is perhaps relative when discussing this candy—hers were quite literally sugar bombs), but I stayed true to the original peanut butter ball dipped in chocolate. Ohioans would be proud. And, yes, leave a little bit of the peanut butter exposed, so that the final candy modestly resembles the horse chestnut from the Buckeye State.

YIELD: 36 TO 42 BUCKEYES

MAKE THE CANDY

In the bowl of a standing mixer fitted with the paddle attachment, beat the cream cheese and peanut butter until combined. Add the graham cracker crumbs and beat on medium speed for 10 seconds. Add the confectioners' sugar and butter. Beat at low speed for 20 seconds to prevent the sugar from spilling over, then gradually increase the speed until the mixture is completely combined. Scrape down the sides and bottom of the bowl and beat again. The mixture will feel slightly dry. Set the peanut butter filling aside while you melt the chocolate.

In the top of a double boiler set over hot water, melt the chocolate, stirring frequently until it is completely smooth. Pour the chocolate into a small, deep bowl. Let it cool to tepid (about 100 degrees F, body temperature) while you shape the peanut butter centers.

ASSEMBLE THE BUCKEYES

Line a sheet pan with parchment paper. Scoop out slightly more than 1 tablespoon's worth of filling and use your hands to form it into a ball. (For uniform balls, use a medium-size melon baller or a very small ice cream scoop with a release mechanism.) Place the ball on the prepared sheet pan and repeat the process until all the filling has been shaped. The balls can sit fairly close to

each other on the sheet, just make sure they are not touching.

One by one, using a fork or large skewer, dip each ball into the chocolate. Roll the ball around from side to side to cover almost the entire peanut butter center, leaving a small part uncovered. Manipulate the buckeye so that the dripping chocolate covers the holes made by the fork. Let the excess chocolate drip back into the bowl and return each chocolate-covered buckeye to the pan. Refrigerate the entire sheet pan for about 30 minutes to set the chocolate before serving.

Buckeyes will keep for up to 3 days, tightly covered, in the refrigerator.

CHOCOLATE PEANUT BUTTER FONDUE

I HAVE MANY ALLEGIANCES TO MANY CANDY BARS AND THEIR ILK. KIT KATS RANK HIGH. As do both plain and peanut M&Ms. And I never travel without a bag of Whoppers or Maltesers. However, I covet the Reese's Peanut Butter Cup above all else. The timeless combo of milk chocolate shell and peanut butter filling is about as boldly American as it gets (my European friends consider peanut butter a strange and unworthy experience). In the 1920s, Mr. Harry Burnett Reese created the candy. His appropriately named company, the H. B. Reese Candy Company, was eventually sold to Hershey's, but the recipe remains relatively unchanged. Our fondue is just another solid reminder that Baked celebrates chocolate and peanut butter unabashedly. Our preferred dipping accompaniment is a brownie—a Baked brownie—but marshmallows, apples, pears, and celery work as well.

ABOUT 2 CUPS

Place the milk chocolate in the top of a double boiler and stir occasionally until it is completely melted and smooth. Add the peanut butter and heavy cream and stir until combined.

Transfer the mixture to your favorite fondue pot and keep it warm. Serve with your choice of dipping items.

Ingredients

8 ounces good-quality milk chocolate, coarsely chopped

1½ cups smooth peanut butter

2 tablespoons heavy cream

Baked Note

This recipe must be made with a high-quality milk chocolate, like Valrhona, Callebaut, or Scharffen Berger. Some of the mass-market brands lack real cocoa butter and use almost no cacao, thereby affecting the consistency of your fondue.

4 tablespoons (½ stick) unsalted butter, cut into 1-inch cubes

⅓ cup firmly packed dark brown sugar

⅓ cup heavy cream

1 teaspoon banana liqueur (or pure vanilla extract)

2 tablespoons dark rum

Pinch cinnamon (optional)

FOR THE FRITTER DOUGH

1¼ cups all-purpose flour, plus more if needed

3 tablespoons firmly packed dark brown sugar

1 teaspoon baking powder

½ teaspoon salt

¼ teaspoon ground allspice

1 teaspoon cinnamon

3 medium ripe bananas

1 tablespoon dark rum

1 teaspoon banana liqueur or pure vanilla extract

1 tablespoon unsalted butter, melted and cooled

Vegetable oil for frying

¼ cup confectioners' sugar

Baked Note

Do not be afraid to fry. It is not as scary as it may initially seem. To keep the mess and time to a minimum, follow these basic rules : 1) Use a high-sided skillet or pan. 2) Do not overcrowd the skillet, or the oil will drop in temperature and your fritters will absorb too much fat. 3) Cool the oil completely before discarding it.

BANANAS FOSTER FRITTERS

AS WITH LIFE IN GENERAL, I HAVE NOTICED THAT MY COOKING LIFE HAS GONE THROUGH VARIOUS PHASES. There was the cake phase, the cookie phase, the anything chocolate and anything caramel phases, and perhaps inevitably, there was the frying phase. I dipped my toe in the frying waters ever so gently with these addictive banana fritters, and from there I started frying everything I could get my hands on: chicken, doughnuts, and dumplings. These fritters are quick, easy, and surprisingly tasty little snacks. The banana flavor really shines through. I last brought them out for an afternoon book-group/coffee-club meeting, and there were many requests for seconds. Treat the rum sauce as optional if you like, but it's well worth the effort. By the by, the rum sauce is awfully tasty on pancakes, French toast, and drizzled on hearty bread puddings.

YIELD: 6 LARGE OR 10 SMALL FRITTERS

MAKE THE RUM DIPPING SAUCE

In a medium saucepan over medium heat, stir the butter and sugar together until smooth. Add the cream and bring to a boil. Remove the pan from the heat and stir in the liqueur, rum, and cinnamon, if using. Set aside until serving time. (The sauce can be made ahead. Allow it to cool, then cover it tightly in plastic wrap and refrigerate. Rewarm it over low heat in a saucepan or microwave it in short 15-second blasts before serving.)

MAKE THE FRITTER DOUGH

In a large bowl, whisk together the flour, brown sugar, baking powder, salt, allspice, and ½ teaspoon of the cinnamon. Use your hands to rub the chunks of sugar into the flour mixture and whisk again (it is okay to have a few chunky sugar pieces remaining).

In another large bowl, mash the bananas with your hands or a heavy spoon and stir in the rum, liqueur, and butter.

Use a rubber spatula to fold the dry ingredients into the banana mixture. The mix should look wet, but it should still hold its shape when scooped into a small ball. If the dough is too thin, keep folding in flour 1 tablespoon at a time until it stiffens up. Refrigerate the dough while the frying oil heats and you prepare the sugar topping.

Pour enough oil into a deep skillet to fill it ¾ inch to 1 inch deep. Slowly heat the oil over medium-high heat until it registers 375 degrees F on a deep-frying thermometer.

While the oil heats, in a small bowl, whisk together the confectioners' sugar and remaining ½ teaspoon cinnamon. Set aside.

FRY THE FRITTERS

Line a plate with a double layer of paper towels and set it near your work area.

Using a small spatula and a small spoon, two spoons, or an ice cream scoop with a release mechanism, drop heaping spoonfuls of dough into the oil. Do not crowd the skillet. Cook until the fritters have browned on one side, 2 to 3 minutes. Using a slotted spoon or tongs, turn them over and continue to cook for another 2 minutes, or until browned. Do not overcook or burn the fritters. Use the slotted spoon to transfer the fritters to the prepared plate and continue frying dough until finished.

Place the fritters on a serving plate and sift the cinnamon sugar over them. Serve immediately with rum dipping sauce.

Ingredients

FOR THE CHOCOLATE CANDY CUPS

16 ounces good-quality dark chocolate (60 to 72%), coarsely chopped

8 ounces good-quality milk chocolate (such as Valrhona or Callebaut), coarsely chopped

FOR THE MARSHMALLOW FILLING

1 envelope (about 2½ teaspoons) unflavored gelatin

1 cup sugar

1 teaspoon pure vanilla extract

⅛ teaspoon salt

Baked Notes

Do not, whatever you do, use supermarket chocolate chips for this recipe. Use high-quality chocolate like Valrhona, Callebaut, or Scharffen Berger. These brands are usually available in block or bar form and can be found online or at most gourmet food stores.

This recipe makes a lot of candies. You can cut the chocolate candy cup recipe in half, keep the marshmallow filling recipe intact, and use larger cup papers (do not use regular cupcake papers) with the end result being a higher ratio of marshmallow to chocolate.

MARSHMALLOW CHOCOLATE CUPS

IT ALL STARTED WITH THE MALLO CUP. Specifically the one manufactured by the Boyer Candy Company in Altoona, Pennsylvania. It was my gateway candy. The fluffy marshmallow filling encased in a dark chocolate candy cup had me hooked from bite number one, and soon I was hoarding and hiding the precious Mallos throughout my room and in the back of the freezer. The Mallo is still decidedly a northeastern treat. It is greatly appreciated within a certain distance from Altoona, and virtually unknown outside of it. I, along with many Mallo enthusiasts, hope to convert the masses and show them the light. In fashioning my own version of the beloved treat, my recipe came to differ from the original in a few ways. It produces a smaller, bite-size candy; the proportion of chocolate to marshmallow is larger; and the shell is made of a mix of dark and milk chocolates. It is easy and fun to make and appropriately delicious. And if you are ever near Altoona, Pennsylvania, it pays to drop by the Boyer factory store for the real thing—I particularly enjoy the discounted "irregulars."

YIELD: 40 TO 60 CANDIES

MAKE THE CHOCOLATE CANDY CUPS

Arrange 30 miniature candy cups (approximately 1 inch in diameter) on a baking sheet. For stability's sake, I suggest using a double layer of cups for each candy (so you will need to buy a total of 60 cups to make 30 candies). This helps your chocolate cup to maintain its shape.

In a large nonreactive metal bowl, combine the chocolates. Set the bowl over a saucepan of simmering water and stir with a rubber spatula until the two chocolates have completely melted together and the mixture is smooth.

Remove the bowl from the simmering water and stir for about 15 seconds to release excess heat. Use either a small spoon or a pastry bag fitted with one of the smallest tips to fill the candy cups just under a quarter full with chocolate. Using a pastry brush, brush the chocolate from the bottom of each cup up the sides to completely cover the inside of the cup with chocolate. Place

the cups in the refrigerator while you make the marshmallow filling. Set the remaining chocolate aside.

PREPARE THE MARSHMALLOW FILLING

Attach a small plain tube tip to a clean pastry bag and set aside.

In the bowl of a standing mixer, sprinkle the gelatin over ⅓ cup cold water.

In a small saucepan over medium heat, gently stir together the sugar and ¼ cup water. Stop stirring and put a candy thermometer in the saucepan. Bring the mixture to a boil over medium-high heat and cook, still without stirring, until it reaches the soft ball stage, 235 degrees F.

Remove the pan from the heat and slowly stream it into the gelatin. Whisk vigorously for about 30 seconds to release excess heat, then place the bowl on the standing mixer fitted with the whisk attachment and mix on medium-high speed for 5 minutes. Add the vanilla and salt and continue to whisk for about 2 minutes longer. You do not want to whisk the marshmallow to soft peaks; it should be slightly looser than that. Working quickly, pour the marshmallow filling into the prepared pastry bag.

ASSEMBLE THE MARSHMALLOW CHOCOLATE CANDY CUPS

Pipe the marshmallow directly into the chocolate cups, filling each one a bit more than three-quarters of the way full. Gently knock the pan to level the filling.

If the reserved chocolate has hardened, set it over simmering water to remelt it. Spoon a top layer of the chocolate onto the marshmallow filling to cover it, gently knock the pan again, and place the cups back in the refrigerator to completely set.

The candy cups will keep, covered, in the refrigerator for up to 4 days. Generally speaking, they can be enjoyed directly from the refrigerator or after a few minutes at room temperature, but they will begin to melt or bloom if left unchilled for too long.

COFFEE ICE CREAM

THE REFRAIN IS FAMILIAR AND CONSISTENT. When people find out I own a bakery, they comment, "I could never own a bakery, I would be too tempted to eat everything all the time." I feel the exact same way about the owners and managers of ice cream parlors. I could easily eat a gallon of ice cream. It is such a problem for me that I often walk the streets of New York taking nonlinear routes to avoid certain ice cream outposts. As ice cream and coffee are two of my favorite vices, it seems natural that I like them even better together. At Baked, we are advocates of the Portland coffee roasters, Stumptown.

YIELD: ONE QUART

MAKE THE COFFEE ICE CREAM

Put the egg yolks in a large heatproof bowl and set aside.

In a medium saucepan, stir together the heavy cream, milk, sugar, salt and instant espresso powder. Bring the mixture to a slow, consistent simmer (just this side of a boil) and remove from heat.

Whisk the egg yolks until just combined, then slowly stream in half of the hot coffee cream mixture while whisking constantly. Transfer the egg mixture back to the medium saucepan containing the other half of the coffee cream mixture. Heat over medium-low heat, stirring constantly, until the mixture is thick enough to coat the back of a spoon (about 175 degrees on an instant-read thermometer).

Remove from heat and strain the mixture through a fine-mesh sieve into a bowl. Whisk in the Kahlúa, and let mixture cool to room temperature.

Press a piece of plastic wrap directly onto the surface of the mixture to prevent a skin from forming. Refrigerate for 4 hours.

Pour into an ice cream machine and freeze, following the manufacturer's directions.

Ingredients

6 egg yolks

1¾ cups heavy cream

2 cups whole milk

¾ cup sugar plus 2 tablespoons

1 teaspoon salt

3 tablespoons instant espresso powder

1 tablespoon Kahlúa

Baked Note

I religiously reiterate the following: Ground espresso is not the same as instant espresso. Ground espresso does not dissolve in liquids, and it produces baked goods and ice cream with a gritty texture while instant espresso dissolves completely resulting in smooth textured baked goods and ice cream. I use the Medaglia D'Oro brand of instant espresso powder, and a small jar will last you for many baking cycles.

STRAWBERRY JELL-O SALAD

I WOULD BE REMISS IF I DIDN'T FEATURE THIS RECIPE IN OUR SECOND COOKBOOK OUT-ING. It was discussed with vigor, passion, and enthusiasm as I made my way around America soliciting regional recipe ideas and thoughts from home bakers. Oddly, Jell-O salad is nearly impossible to pin down to one region. Many locales lay claim to some form of the dessert. The confusion of ownership probably resides in the many twists and turns the recipe has made from generation to generation. Generally speaking, I found the Jell-O salad of the West to be more of a "mix it all together and add pineapple bits" affair, while the Jell-O salad of the East remains a clearly layered, strawberry only, dessert. This version is pretty much a facsimile of an original. A crunchy pretzel crust holds a layer of cream cheese frosting topped with thick strawberry Jell-O. In theory, it shouldn't work, but it does. I did not add any flourishes, and I did not attempt to dress it up for mass consumption. You are either a Jell-O Salad fan or a hater. Decide for yourself.

YIELD: ONE 9-BY-13-INCH DESSERT OR
ABOUT 15 GENEROUS SERVINGS

MAKE THE JELL-O LAYER

Prepare the Jell-O according to the package directions. Add the sliced strawberries and refrigerate until it is partially set (this takes about 45 minutes to 1 hour depending on the depth and type of vessel you use to chill the Jell-O). Make the other parts of the recipe while you wait for the Jell-O to nearly set.

MAKE THE PRETZEL CRUST

Preheat the oven to 325 degrees F. Butter the sides and bottom of a 9-by-13-inch baking pan, or spray it with nonstick cooking spray.

In a food processor, pulse the pretzels into coarse crumbs. Do not overprocess into a powder—if anything, err on the side of having a few chunkier pretzel pieces (it's simply my preference). Alternatively, crush the pretzels with the bottom of a metal baking cup.

In a medium saucepan, melt the butter over low heat. Whisk in the brown sugar and remove from the heat. Stir in the pretzel pieces until combined

Ingredients

FOR THE JELL-O LAYER

1 (6-ounce) package strawberry Jell-O

2 cups fresh strawberries (about 14 ounces), sliced

FOR THE PRETZEL CRUST

8 ounces salty pretzels (about 4 cups)

¾ cup (1½ sticks) unsalted butter, cut into ½-inch pieces

2 tablespoons firmly packed dark brown sugar

FOR THE CREAM CHEESE LAYER

1 (8 ounce package) cream cheese, at room temperature

1 cup sugar

¾ cup heavy cream

Baked Note

Jell-O Salad requires you to leave your culinary criticism and classically honed foodie personality at the door. This ill-named dessert requires a completely open mind. Feel free to swap out the strawberry Jell-O for any other fruit flavor, like orange, lemon, or lime. I have yet to try a chocolate gelatin or a chocolate pudding layer in place of the strawberry layer, but I am fairly certain it will work just fine.

and turn the mixture out into the prepared pan. Use your hands or the back of a large spoon to press the mixture into the bottom of the pan, but do not press it up the sides. Bake the crust for 10 minutes, then set it aside to cool completely.

MAKE THE CREAM CHEESE LAYER

Put the cream cheese and sugar in the bowl of a standing mixer fitted with the paddle attachment. Beat on medium speed until well combined.

In a clean bowl, whip the cream, either by hand or using the standing mixer with the whip attachment, until soft peaks form. Use a rubber spatula to fold the whipped cream into the cream cheese mixture.

ASSEMBLE THE STRAWBERRY JELL-O SALAD

Spread the cream cheese mixture over the cooled crust. Chill for 5 minutes in the refrigerator. Pour the almost-set Jell-O over the cream cheese layer to cover. Refrigerate the dessert for 2 about hours or more to set before serving.

The Jell-O salad can be stored, tightly covered and refrigerated, for up to 3 days.

THE NO-BAKE PEANUT BUTTER COOKIE

THERE SEEMS TO HAVE BEEN A MOMENT IN AMERICAN HISTORY WHEN EVERY MOTHER MADE A VERSION OF THIS NO-BAKE COOKIE FOR HER CHILDREN. A large number of the people contributing ideas to this book submitted a version of this dessert and they all claimed to have watched (or helped) Mom make it. Perhaps the ease with which this recipe comes together explains its ubiquity. It was something every mother could make, regardless of time constraints or baking ability. It is surprisingly good, and well textured. It is fully capable of inspiring a classic midnight craving—I found myself sneaking them from the fridge along with a glass of milk. I am hesitant to call it a cookie, though, as it isn't baked, but you can call it whatever you like.

YIELD: ABOUT 36 COOKIES

Line two baking sheets with parchment paper.

In a heavy saucepan over medium heat, stir together the milk, sugar, cocoa powder, and butter until the butter is melted and the sugar is dissolved. Bring the mixture to a boil, stop stirring, and boil for a full 90 seconds. Remove the pan from the heat and add the peanut butter, oats, and vanilla. Stir until the mixture is combined.

Use a small ice scream scoop with a release mechanism or, alternatively, a tablespoon to drop the no-bake cookies onto the baking sheet (leave some room around them; they will spread). Let the cookies cool, then refrigerate them for at least 1 hour. They can be eaten directly from the refrigerator or at room temperature.

Store the cookies between layers of parchment paper in a tightly sealed container for up to 3 days.

Ingredients

½ cup whole milk

2 cups sugar

¼ cup dark unsweetened cocoa powder (like Valrhona)

½ cup (1 stick) butter, cut into ½-inch cubes, softened

1 cup chunky peanut butter

3 cups rolled oats

1 teaspoon pure vanilla extract

Baked Note

Yes, you can replace the chunky peanut butter with smooth. And yes, you can use natural peanut butter instead—but if you do, add about ⅓ cup more oats to absorb the extra oil.

4 to 6 ounces vanilla wafers, depending
on how thick you want to make your
wafer layer

2½ cups fresh blueberries

¼ cup Grand Marnier

1 teaspoon orange juice

¾ cup heavy cream

1 teaspoon confectioners' sugar, sifted

Freshly grated zest of 1 orange for garnish

Baked Note

Obviously, this book is not written for the
diet-minded; however, this recipe can
easily be given a healthier spin. Simply
replace the whipped heavy cream with
about 1½ to 2 cups of yogurt. The dessert
will be equally delicious, though the
yogurt is slightly heavier.

SIMPLE BLUEBERRY PARFAITS

MAINE IS THE SINGLE LARGEST PRODUCER OF LOWBUSH BLUEBERRIES IN THE WORLD, AND THAT ALONE IS REASON ENOUGH TO VISIT THE STATE. Prime blueberry season, August through September, also happens to coincide exactly with the perfect time for a road trip to Maine. It is dry and cool and sunny, while the rest of the East Coast is humid, hot, and insufferable. I highly recommend a drive along the coast with many stop-offs at the roadside farm stands filled with blueberries. It's the perfect way to end a long, sticky summer. I buy them by the bagful, and September becomes a month of blueberry muffins, blueberry waffles, and blueberry parfaits.

YIELD: **4 SERVINGS**

Choose four clear, wide-mouthed glasses for serving. Put the vanilla wafers in a food processor and pulse them into coarse crumbs.

In a small saucepan, combine 1¼ cups of the blueberries and the Grand Marnier. Cook over medium heat until the blueberries break down, about 5 minutes. Let them cool to room temperature. (If you're in a hurry, put the mixture in the refrigerator to cool it quickly.)

In the bowl of a standing mixer fitted with the whisk attachment, whip the cream on medium speed for 1 minute. Sprinkle the confectioners' sugar over the cream, turn the mixer to high, and beat until soft peaks form.

Add ¾ cup of the fresh blueberries and the orange juice to the room-temperature blueberry syrup and stir until combined.

Sprinkle about a tablespoon of the crumbled vanilla wafers to cover the bottom of each glass, top with a heaping tablespoonful of the blueberry mixture, then top that with a dollop of whipped cream. Continue to layer until you fill the glasses or until you run out of ingredients. Garnish with the remaining ½ cup blueberries and finish each parfait with a sprinkle of orange zest. Serve immediately.

CARAMEL POPCORN
WITH PEANUTS AND CHOCOLATE

BY AND LARGE, I HAVE NEVER BEEN DRAWN TO POPCORN. It is a snack that I rarely think about and only eat a bit reluctantly, if someone offers me his or her bucket at the movies. It was not until Renato introduced me to the voodoo-like nature of homemade caramel popcorn that I understood the allure. The otherwise average kernels turn into something else entirely. The salty peanuts, crunchy popcorn, and dark chocolate form an otherworldly snack that has the overall effect of encouraging epic consumption and borderline hysteria. Finally, since the yield on this recipe is rather large, we encourage you to get out cellophane bags and decorative bows and use a portion of your caramel popcorn for gifts. It makes a great present and will save you a few otherwise unavoidable calories.

YIELD: 24 CUPS

If you are starting with kernels, pop them using any method you prefer and let them cool. (We like a hot-air popper.) Preheat the oven to 250 degrees F. Place the popcorn in a large roasting pan. Line a sheet pan with parchment paper.

In a medium saucepan over low heat, start to melt the butter. Add the brown sugar, corn syrup, and molasses, and stir gently with a heatproof spatula. Continue to cook over medium heat, stirring only occasionally, until the mixture starts to boil. Clip a candy thermometer to the side of the pan and bring the syrup to the soft-ball stage, approximately 240 degrees F. Remove the pan from the heat and stir in the salt, the baking soda, and vanilla. Pour the caramel over the popcorn in large streams, then sprinkle with the peanuts. Use your spatula to fold the popcorn until it is completely coated with caramel.

Place the roasting pan in the oven and bake for 15 minutes. Use a spatula to lift, flip, and coat the popcorn in the warm caramel, then continue baking for another 20 minutes. Cool the caramel popcorn in the pan for 5 minutes and transfer it to the lined sheet pan. Cool for approximately 15 minutes and drizzle the milk chocolate and dark chocolate in crisscross patterns over the top. Let the chocolate set before breaking the popcorn into serving-size pieces. Store in an airtight container for up to 1 week.

Ingredients

1 cup unpopped kernels or 24 cups popped corn

1 cup (2 sticks) unsalted butter, cut into chunks

2 cups firmly packed dark brown sugar

½ cup light corn syrup

2 tablespoons unsulfured molasses

½ teaspoon salt

¾ teaspoon baking soda

1½ teaspoons pure vanilla extract

1¼ cups salted peanuts

8 ounces good-quality milk chocolate, melted and tempered (page 190)

8 ounces good-quality dark chocolate (60 to 72%), melted and tempered (page 190)

Baked Note

This caramel popcorn virtually begs for chocolate, but if you don't want to go through the trouble and time of tempering it, we completely understand. You can just leave it out. Additionally, this recipe was adapted from none other than my Aunt Judy, by way of a Land O'Lakes Butter recipe that she has kept for untold years.

In this book, I use tempered chocolate in the delicious caramel popcorn, but tempering also comes in handy for homemade truffles, dipping macaroons, and making molded chocolate candy bars and novelties.

The process of tempering chocolate is a lot less complicated than explaining the science of tempering chocolate; however, I feel obligated to give you a brief intro:

What is going on?

There are many methods of tempering chocolate, but each is accomplished through a process of melting, cooling, and agitating. Our favorite method is to seed the chocolate. Here, a portion of already tempered chocolate is added to melted chocolate. This helps stimulate the formation of stable beta crystals—or, to put it simply, reduces the temperature of the melted chocolate and helps it come to temper.

Getting started

It is much easier to temper in a cool kitchen. Measure out 1 pound of chocolate—dark or milk, depending on the recipe —and chop into small chunks. I prefer a couverture chocolate that contains at least 32 percent cocoa butter, as it is thinner when melted and ideal for dipping.

Tempering

Place about a quarter of the chocolate in a bowl and set aside. Put the remainder in a large heat-proof bowl and place over a pot of simmering water. Melt the chocolate until an instant-read thermometer placed in the middle of the bowl reads 120 degrees F.

Remove the bowl from the heat and add the reserved chopped chocolate. With a rubber spatula, stir the chocolate vigorously without stopping until it has completely melted and cooled to a temperature of 80 degrees F. The chocolate should thicken considerably.

Place the bowl of chocolate back over the simmering water and stir with a spatula. If you are using dark chocolate, bring it to a temperature between 86 and 90 degrees F. If you are using milk chocolate, a temperature between 84 and 87 degrees F works best.

Test the chocolate to make sure it has reached a full temper. Dip a small metal spatula into the chocolate and place it on the counter. The chocolate should begin to set in 3 to 5 minutes and have a satiny shine, without streaks. If the chocolate has not set after 5 minutes or it looks speckled or streaked, you should continue to agitate the chocolate with the spatula until it is properly tempered.

When your chocolate is tempered, you may begin using the chocolate. Keep in mind that tempered chocolate sets up quickly. If you notice the chocolate in your bowl is beginning to harden, place it back over the simmering water to reheat, but only for a few seconds.

CLASSIC CARAMEL SAUCE
(FOR COFFEE CAKE AND THE LIKE)

THIS CLASSIC AND EASY CARAMEL SAUCE IS A COMPONENT OF OUR CARAMEL APPLE CAKE (PAGE 138). It is also a perfect stand-alone recipe and can be used on all manner of cakes, ice creams, and quick breads. This recipe makes more than you actually need for the Caramel Apple Cake itself, so I encourage you to find a tasty use for the leftovers.

YIELD: ABOUT 2 CUPS

Ingredients

1½ cups sugar

¼ cup corn syrup

½ cup (1 stick) of butter, softened, cut into ½-inch cubes

1½ cups heavy cream

In a medium saucepan with high sides, combine the sugar and corn syrup with ½ cup water. Stir the mixture gently so you don't slosh any of it up the sides of the pan. Turn the heat to medium-high and continue stirring until the sugar dissolves. Increase heat to high, stop stirring, and allow the mixture to boil. Once it begins to turn a rich caramel color (if you don't want to eyeball it, take the caramel to 300 degrees F on a candy thermometer), remove it from the heat, add the butter and cream, and stir until combined.

You can save the caramel sauce, tightly covered, in the refrigerator for up to 1 week. Let it come to room temperature before using it on cakes, ice creams, or quick breads.

If you want a warm topping, heat the caramel sauce in short bursts in the microwave or in the top of a double boiler.

1 tablespoon bourbon

1 vanilla bean

4 ounces good-quality milk chocolate

2 large egg yolks

2 large eggs

¼ cup heavy cream

½ cup sugar

⅓ cup cornstarch, sifted

½ teaspoon salt

3 cups whole milk

1 tablespoon unsalted butter

Simple Whipped Cream to serve (optional, page 159)

Baked Note

If you prefer to make just vanilla pudding, omit the milk chocolate. If you wish to make just the chocolate pudding, double the milk chocolate and omit the vanilla bean and bourbon. And, of course, ignore the layering instructions.

VANILLA BEAN AND CHOCOLATE BUDINO

TO TELL YOU THE TRUTH, BUDINO IS JUST A FANCY ITALIAN WORD FOR PUDDING. Good old American pudding is pretty much indistinguishable from the more debonair-sounding budino—but this is a debate I avoid with certain family members. I have named this dessert in deference to them, and it is a really great pudding.

Made-from-scratch pudding is superior to the packaged variety in every imaginable way and in theory, it won't take you much longer to make. I prefer a richer pudding experience, pudding slightly thicker and slightly deeper than average. Though I am partial to dark chocolate, I think the milk chocolate in this dessert works extremely well layered against the creamy vanilla bean pudding. I suggest serving this in small glass cups—a little goes a long way, and you'll probably want to show off the layers. And remember, if anybody asks, this is a budino, not a pudding.

← YIELD: 8 SERVINGS →

Choose eight small wide-mouthed glasses for serving.

Put the bourbon in a medium heatproof bowl. Cut the vanilla bean in half lengthwise, and, using the tip of a knife or small spoon, scrape the seeds into the bourbon. Discard the vanilla bean and stir the mixture to combine.

Place the milk chocolate in another medium heatproof bowl.

In a third heatproof bowl, whisk together the egg yolks, whole eggs, and cream.

In a medium saucepan, whisk together the sugar, cornstarch, and salt. Whisk in the milk. Cook the mixture over medium-high heat until it just begins to boil, stirring occasionally. Whisking constantly, pour a third of the milk mixture over the egg mixture, then add another third of the hot milk mixture. Transfer the tempered egg mixture to the saucepan with the milk mixture and, whisking constantly, bring it to a boil. Cook for 2 to 3 minutes, or until the pudding is very thick.

Pour half of the pudding over the vanilla bean mixture and half over the milk chocolate. Add half of the butter to the vanilla mixture and whisk vigorously to cool the pudding slightly. Add the remaining butter to the chocolate mixture and again whisk vigorously to release the heat.

ASSEMBLE THE DESSERT

Divide the vanilla pudding among the serving glasses. Chill them for 20 minutes. While the vanilla pudding is in the refrigerator, whisk the chocolate pudding every 5 minutes to release excess heat.

Spoon the chocolate layer on top of the vanilla, cover (see Sidebar below), and chill the puddings until firm, about 2 hours, before serving.

Top with whipped cream, if you like, and serve immediately.

The puddings can be stored, tightly covered, in the refrigerator for up to 2 days. Do not add the whipped cream until you are ready to serve them.

SKIN OR NO SKIN

Silly me, I just assumed that nobody wants a skin (you know—that thick, continuous top layer) on pudding. Well, I was dead wrong. In fact, I have met just as many skin pudding people as no-skin pudding people, and each side is quite vocal.

Either version is easy to accomplish. If you want a skin, wrap the pudding vessel tightly before refrigerating it and do not let the plastic wrap come in contact with the top of the pudding. If you do not want a skin, gently press the plastic wrap down onto the surface of the pudding, then refrigerate.

MERINGUE MUSHROOMS,
OR SHANDI'S CANDIES

THEORETICALLY, I AM A YOLK MAN. I CAN WORK THROUGH A HILL OF EGG YOLKS IN A MATTER OF DAYS IF I AM FEELING GAME FOR A RUN OF RICH CHOCOLATE PUDDINGS AND VELVETY ICE CREAMS. Inevitably, I am left with a surplus of egg whites. And when I have extra egg whites, I make meringues. A meringue is a simple cloudlike confection of whipped egg whites and sugar, and it is likely they have been part of the baking pantheon for hundreds of years. They are crunchy, light, and very sweet, a lovely little afternoon snack. Our meringue mushrooms are a featured accompaniment to our Stump de Noël (page 144), but I encourage you not to limit your meringue making to holiday cake decor. Make them any time you have leftover egg whites (assuming you won't be using them for Angel frosting). It should be noted that these meringues are dedicated to a kind customer, Shandi, who had a limitless appetite for these candies.

YIELD: ABOUT 2 DOZEN (SMALL) MUSHROOMS

Preheat the oven to 200 degrees F. Line two sheet pans with parchment paper.

Whisk the egg whites and sugar together in the heat proof bowl of a standing mixer. Set the bowl over a saucepan of simmering water (double boiler method). Cook, whisking constantly, until the sugar is completely dissolved and the mixture registers 140 degrees F on an instant-read thermometer, 6 to 8 minutes.

Transfer the bowl to a standing mixer fitted with the whisk attachment. Beat it on high speed until stiff peaks form. Add the cream of tartar when the mixture begins to thicken, or after 3 minutes. Keep beating for another minute or so until stiff peaks hold.

Fill a pastry bag fitted with a large round tip with the meringue. To make the caps, hold the pastry bag close to the parchment paper–lined pan and pipe out a small dome (about a tablespoon) of meringue, pulling up at the very end of piping to give your cap some height.

To form the mushroom stems, hold the bag close to the parchment paper and pipe the meringue, pulling up as you go, into small cone shapes. Make the same number of stems as caps.

Place the pans in the oven and bake the meringue pieces for 90 minutes, rotating the baking sheets halfway through the baking time. Turn off the oven, prop the door slightly open, and leave the meringues in place for at least 2 hours longer, or overnight.

ASSEMBLE THE MERINGUE MUSHROOMS

Turn the caps over and use a toothpick to make a tiny hole large enough to fit the tip of the stem into. Fill the hole with a tiny bit of white chocolate. Gently press the stem into place and allow the chocolate to set. Sift cocoa powder over the assembled mushrooms.

DRESS UP YOUR STUMP

The Stump de Noël (page 144-146) is a thing of beauty regardless of whether it is stark-raving naked or wrapped up in baubles and bling. If you wish to add some adornment to your "Stump" or any other holiday treat, try out this simple recipe for sugared cranberries and sugared rosemary.

¼ cup superfine sugar *¾ cup fresh cranberries*
1 cup granulated sugar *10 rosemary sprigs*
1 cinnamon stick

Line a half-sheet pan with parchment paper. Place the superfine sugar in a small bowl.

In a medium saucepan, stir together 1 cup of water with the sugar, then add the cinnamon stick. Bring the mixture to a boil over medium-high heat and stir until the sugar is completely dissolved. Remove from the heat and pour into a heatproof, wide-mouthed bowl. Let the liquid cool for a few minutes, then remove the cinnamon stick.

Drop the cranberries in the syrup and stir to coat the cranberries completely. Remove the cranberries, a few at a time, with a slotted spoon (tap the spoon to release excess syrup) and drop them in the superfine sugar. Toss the cranberries in the sugar to coat completely, and place on the parchment paper to dry. Repeat the above process with the rosemary. Decorate "the Stump" at will.

2 cups light corn syrup

1 cup granulated sugar

1 cup firmly packed light brown sugar

2 cups heavy cream

⅔ cup condensed milk

½ cup (1 stick) unsalted butter, at room
temperature, cut into cubes

2 teaspoons pure vanilla extract

1 teaspoon sea salt or fleur de sel

Baked Note

It is important to make sure your candy
thermometer is accurate before making
caramels (or, really, any candy). A batch
of ruined caramels is annoying and
expensive. If you are unsure or if you
haven't used your thermometer in some
time, boil some water in a medium pot,
clip the thermometer to the side of the
pot, and wait 5 minutes. The thermometer
should read 212 degrees F.

SOFT CANDY CARAMELS

MOM WAS RESOLUTE. HALLOWEEN WAS HER FAVORITE HOLIDAY, AND SHE WAS UNYIELDING IN THE CANDY SELECTION. The shelves of the grocery store were stocked, literally bulging, with eye-catching displays of my favorite candy bars and confections, wrapped in special Halloween-themed packaging and perfectly bite-size (or two-bite-size) for trick-or-treaters. Mom ignored these, barely acknowledged my pleadings for the Hershey's multipack, and moved quickly to the less-colorful part of the candy aisle. She always made a beeline for the caramel candies, Brach's maybe, the kind wrapped tightly in white wax paper. The kind that stuck in your teeth and tasted overwhelmingly like vanilla. The kind of thing I didn't want Mom to give out on Halloween.

Over the years, I grew to appreciate the caramel candies and even anticipated their presence in our house; however, the homemade version is infinitely better. These soft candy caramels have a pleasingly smooth texture and the smoky, buttery dark caramel taste that is absent in their mass-produced counterparts.

YIELD: ABOUT 70 CARAMELS

Lightly spray a 9-inch square baking pan with nonstick cooking spray and line it with aluminum foil, allowing the foil to just overhang on the sides. Lightly coat the foil with nonstick cooking spray.

In a medium saucepan, gently stir together the corn syrup and sugars along with ¼ cup water. Set the saucepan over low heat and continue to stir gently until the sugars dissolve (avoid sloshing the sides of the pan). Once the sugar has dissolved, clip a candy thermometer to the side of the pan, turn the heat up to medium-high, and wait for the mixture to reach 240 to 245 degrees F, about 7 minutes. Keep a watchful eye on the temperature while you proceed with the next step—you do not want it to exceed 250 degrees F.

Meanwhile, in a small saucepan, stir together the cream and condensed milk and set over medium heat. Gently warm the mixture; do not let it boil.

Once the sugar mixture turns amber, remove it from the heat and stir in the butter and warm milk mixture until completely combined (be careful about splattering; it usually bubbles up when you add the milk mixture). Place the pan back on medium heat, stop stirring, and bring the mixture back to 245 to 250 degrees F.

Remove the pan from the heat, stir in the vanilla and salt, and pour the caramel into the prepared pan. Allow the candy to set for 8 hours, or overnight.

CUT AND WRAP THE SOFT CANDY CARAMELS

Place a sheet of parchment over the caramel and invert it onto a cutting surface. Remove the aluminum foil.

Spray a chef's knife with nonstick cooking spray or carefully rub a tiny bit of vegetable shortening along the blade. Cut the caramels into 1 by ½-inch rectangles, and immediately wrap them in wax paper or candy papers. Twist the ends of the papers to resemble old-school candies. Distribute with brio to friends and family.

The caramels will keep in an airtight container at room temperature for up to 10 days.

Ingredients

2 cups whole hazelnuts

1¼ cups confectioners' sugar, sifted

⅓ cup dark unsweetened cocoa powder, (like Valrhona)

½ teaspoon pure vanilla extract

Dash salt

3 to 4 tablespoons hazelnut oil (or alternatively vegetable oil)

Baked Note

This recipe can be used to replace the Nutella in the hazelnut scones (page 32). Because the homemade version lacks the spreadable consistency of the original, though, make sure to bring it to room temperature and stir in an extra teaspoon of hazelnut oil beforehand.

CHOCOLATE HAZELNUT SPREAD

I AM A MAN OF GOOD INTENTIONS. I HAVE GRAND IDEAS ABOUT RAISING MY OWN CHICKENS (FOR EGGS), CHURNING MY OWN BUTTER, AND GRINDING MY OWN SPICES ON AN AS-NEEDED BASIS. I would also like to make homemade Nutella more often. Unfortunately, I am still without my own chickens, and I rarely churn my own butter—but I have reorganized my spice drawer with a tilt toward the fresh, and I have been making this chocolate hazelnut spread repeatedly for a wide swath of friends. I am still addicted to the jarred stuff. I still impulsively place at least two tubs of Nutella in my grocery cart without conscious thought, but I also thoroughly enjoy the homemade version. Adapted from the brilliant blogger Jessica Su of Su Good Sweets, it is thicker and a bit richer than Nutella, and it is heavenly. I am still uncertain whether it is less expensive (after all, hazelnuts are pricey), but it is well worth the effort. Serve it on toast, bananas, graham crackers, pancakes, tucked inside a crepe, warmed and poured on ice cream, or with almost anything else you dream of.

YIELD: APPROXIMATELY 1½ CUPS

Preheat the oven to 350 degrees F. Line a baking sheet with parchment paper.

Spread the hazelnuts across the prepared pan in a single layer and toast them in the oven for 8 minutes. Toss the nuts, then toast them for another 5 to 6 minutes, until they are fragrant and have turned a dark brown. Let the nuts cool completely.

Remove the skins from the cooled nuts by placing them in a damp towel and rubbing them together. Discard the skins.

Place the nuts in the bowl of a food processor and process for 3 to 5 minutes, until the nuts liquefy and become buttery. Scrape down the bowl and process for 30 seconds longer.

Add the sugar, cocoa powder, vanilla, salt, and 3 tablespoons of the hazelnut oil, and process again for about 1 more minute, or until the mixture is smooth and spreadable. If it is too thick, add more hazelnut oil, a teaspoon at a time, until the right consistency is achieved.

Use the spread immediately or store it in the refrigerator, in a tightly sealed container, for up to 2 weeks. Initially, the spread will be wet and thin (perfect for dipping). However it will thicken considerably in the refrigerator and have a consistency akin to chilled peanut butter. For spreading purposes, remove from the refrigerator 15 minutes before using, it will be more pliable and spreadable.

Acknowledgments

Baked Explorations was a little bit of a beast—a beast that we loved and nurtured, but a monster all the same. Without the help of a great circle of friends and acquaintances, we may have been entirely consumed.

First, a much deserved special thank you to Eric Wolitzky. He is a talented pastry chef, a studious technician, and such a great interpreter of Baked dreams that we thought he might be living in our brains. His version of the Mississippi Mud is to be blamed for our sudden involuntary weight gain.

Also, big love to Alison Fargis, agent extraordinaire. At once, protective sister, kick-ass baker, and avid reader—the book trade is a better world with her in it.

Both of our editors, Luisa Weiss and Natalie Kaire, deserve a quiet place in Heaven for dealing with our endless missed deadlines, our severe misgivings about letting a recipe go, and our haphazard self-editing process. Free cakes to you both for life—we appreciate you both more than you know. And thanks to everyone else at STC for giving Baked a tactile voice especially Alissa Faden for designing the heck out of this book.

A hearty thanks to the small army of testers who took the time to spin an endless array of butter, eggs, sugar and chocolate into gold: Liz Moore, Rachel Boller (forever in my heart as the cake lady), Joann Tamburro, Clay Smith, Lianna Allday, Gretchen Lewis (aka multi-tasker), Larry Lewis (aka swell dad), Nancy Mongiovi, and Jessie Sheehan (aka Brookie Queen).

Matt Holbein deserves special recognition as roadie/crew member/all-around Baked believer. Sven Wiedmann for his persistent patience. Grace (mom) Poliafito for the cake. And Rafi Avaramovitz gets billing for his consistent belief. As always Martha Stewart holds a special place in our hearts for giving Baked its first big break.

The lush photos are served up by the same snazzy crew from the first cookbook, including Tina Rupp who can sex up Jell-O Salad like no one's business, and prop-mistress Leslie Seigel.

We have to thank the coolest set of employees, past and present, to ever grace a bakery. We would like to thank them all, but special props to Melissa Fritz—our southern Bakemistress, Jessica Bacchus, Stephanie Francis (Helga), Stephanie Whitten (Vera), Kristine Moberg (can we come back to SD?), and Lesli Heffler. Lesli was never a proper employee, much to our consternation, but we always wanted her to be and she is a genius food stylist.

If we forget anyone, please hunt us down and ask us for brownies.

Matt and Nato

CANDY

ECONOMY CANDY
108 Rivington Street
New York, NY 10002
800. 352-4544
www.economycandy.com
Maltesers, Milk Chocolate-covered Peanuts, and a multitude of other candies and choco-lates.

KOPPERS CHOCOLATE
800.325.0026
www.kopperschocolate.com
Malted Milk Balls (Whoppers), Chocolate-covered Peanuts available in bulk quantities.

CHOCOLATE AND OTHER SPECIALTY INGREDIENTS

CALLEBAUT CHOCOLATE
www.callebaut.com

DIVINE CHOCOLATE
202-332-8913
www.divinechocolateusa.com
Fair Trade quality chocolate and cocoa.

JAQUES TORRES
212.414.2462
350 Hudson Street
New York, NY 10014
www.mrchocolate.com

SCHARFFEN BERGER
866.608.6944
Available in most grocery/specialty stores.
www.scharffenberger.com

VALRHONA CHOCOLATE
www.valrhona-chocolate.com
Also available in many specialty stores.

WHOLE FOODS
Organic foods as well as a great variety of high-grade chocolates. Go to www.wholefoods-markets.com for locations in your area.

NEILSEN MASSEY
800-525-7873
www.nielsenmassey.com
Great source for Vanilla Bean Paste and Coffee Extract (and of course, Pure Vanilla Extract)

SALTWORKS
800-353-7258
www.saltworks.us
Wide variety of salts sold in bulk portions.

ANSON MILLS
803-467-4122
www.ansonmills.com
Stone ground grits. Get some.

BOBS RED MILL
800-553-2258
www.bobsredmill.com
Grits and specialty flours.

INDIA TREE
800-369-4848
www.indiatree.com
Great resource for specialty sugars.

KITCHEN & BAKING EQUIPMENT

CRATE & BARREL
Call 800.967.6696 for store locations in your area.
www.crateandbarrel.com

JB PRINCE
800.473.0577
www.jbprince.com

KING ARTHUR FLOUR BAKERS CATALOGUE
Norwich, VT 05005
800.827.6836
www.kingarthurflour.com

KITCHENAID APPLIANCES
Call 800.334.6889 for a KitchenAid distribu-tor in your area.
kitchenaid.com

NEW YORK CAKE & BAKE
800.942.2539
56 West 22nd Street
New York, NY 10010
www.nycake.com
A fantastic resource for the New York-based baker. Pans, tools and decorating equipment.

PFEIL & HOLING
58-15 Northern Blvd.
Woodside, NY 11377
800.247.7955
www.cakedeco.com
Decorating supplies sold in bulk.

SUR LA TABLE
Call 800.243.0852 for store locations in your area.
www.surlatable.com

WILLIAMS-SONOMA
Call 800.541.1262 for store locations in your area.
www.williams-sonoma.com

Conversion Chart

Weight Equivalents: The metric weights given in this chart are not exact equivalents, but have been rounded up or down slightly to make measuring easier.

Volume Equivalents: These are not exact equivalents for American cups and spoons, but have been rounded up or down slightly to make measuring easier.

AVOIRDUPOIS	METRIC
¼ oz	7 g
½ oz	15 g
1 oz	30 g
2 oz	60 g
3 oz	90 g
4 oz	115 g
5 oz	150 g
6 oz	175 g
7 oz	200 g
8 oz (½ lb)	225 g
9 oz	250 g
10 oz	300 g
11 oz	325 g
12 oz	350 g
13 oz	375 g
14 oz	400 g
15 oz	425 g
16 oz (1 lb)	450 g
1 ½ lb	750 g
2 lb	900 g
2 ¼ lb	1 kg
3 lb	1.4 kg
4 lb	1.8 kg

AMERICAN	METRIC	IMPERIAL
¼ tsp	1.2 ml	
½ tsp	2.5 ml	
1 tsp	5.0 ml	
½ Tbsp (1.5 tsp)	7.5 ml	
1 Tbsp (3 tsp)	15 ml	
¼ cup (4 Tbsp)	60 ml	2 fl oz
⅓ cup (5 Tbsp)	75 ml	2.5 fl oz
½ cup (8 Tbsp)	125 ml	4 fl oz
⅔ cup (10 Tbsp)	150 ml	5 fl oz
¾ cup (12 Tbsp)	175 ml	6 fl oz
1 cup (16 Tbsp)	250 ml	8 fl oz
1¼ cups	300 ml	10 fl oz (½ pint)
1½ cups	350 ml	12 fl oz
2 cups (1 pint)	500 ml	16 fl oz
2½ cups	625 ml	20 fl oz (1 pint)
1 quart	1 liter	32 fl oz

OVEN MARK	F	C	GAS
Very cool	250–275	130–140	½–1
Cool	300	150	2
Warm	325	170	3
Moderate	350	180	4
Moderately hot	375	190	5
	400	200	6
Hot	425	220	7
	450	230	8
Very hot	475	250	9

Index

Recipe Index

Published in 2010 by Stewart, Tabori & Chang
An imprint of ABRAMS

Text copyright © 2010 Matt Lewis and Renato Poliafito
Illustrations/photographs copyright © 2010 Tina Rupp

Library of Congress Cataloging-in-Publication Data
Lewis, Matt.
Baked explorations : classic American desserts revisited / Matt Lewis,
Renato Poliafito ; photography by Tina Rupp.
p. cm.
ISBN 978-1-58479-850-7 (alk. paper)
1. Baking. 2. Desserts. 3. Baked (Bakery) I. Poliafito, Renato. II.
Title.
TX765.L673 2010
641.8'6--dc22
2010016610

Editor: Natalie Kaire
Designer: Alissa Faden
Production Manager: Tina Cameron

The text of this book was primarily composed in Asteroid, Century Expanded, Pabst, and Sackers.

Printed and bound in Hong Kong, China
10 9 8 7 6 5 4 3 2 1

Stewart, Tabori & Chang books are available at special discounts when purchased in quantity for premiums and promotions as well as fundraising or educational use. Special editions can also be created to specification. For details, contact specialsales@abramsbooks.com or the address below.

ABRAMS
THE ART OF BOOKS SINCE 1949
115 West 18th Street
New York, NY 10011
www.abramsbooks.com